© 2010 Antinous Press © 2010 Hy Abady

All rights reserved. No part of this book may be reproduced in any manner in any media, or transmitted by any means whatsoever, electronic or mechanical (including photocopy, film or video recording, internet posting, or any information storage and retrieval system), without the prior written permission of the publisher.

Published in the United States
First Edition, 2010

ISBN-13: 978-0-615-38002-5

April, 2012

BACK IN THE STAR AGAIN

Matthew

HY ABADY

Hope you have as much fun reading these stories as I've had writing them — Enjoy

Hy Abady

A
ANTINOUS PRESS

A Date With Andy	1
What's a Supermodel To Do?	11
South of Highway Robbery	17
Renée and Me	26
Forgiveness, Hampton Style	33
My Night With Nora	41
The Deal With Dogs	47
My Two Dads	53
If You Want to Feel 100	61
Puccini, Part 2	67
What I Do	72
Back in The Star Again	136

A Date With Andy

You wait for those phone calls to come that will change your life. Once in a while, you pick up the receiver to see if the wire has gone dead. Then you wait some more. While you wait, you start to think that those calls only happen to other people. Or to liars. You stop believing the people who say they met so-and-so and nothing since has been the same. Or they've seen such-and-such a movie and destiny was changed.

Still, I kept waiting. Then, on a drizzly April day, it rang for me. It had all the earmarks. A man on the other end, a Stephen Greenberg, had gotten my name from a friend in the advertising business because that friend thought I'd be interested in meeting Andy Warhol. Over dinner at a downtown restaurant. As part of a new idea that he or

Back in the Star Again

Andy had dreamt up called: Blind Date of the '80s.

I should have been skeptical at the start—anything with 'of the '80s' tacked on after it smelled of disaster. To try and give the lousy decade some significance while it was still painstakingly in progress seemed terribly self-conscious. But because I wanted to believe, I believed. There I was, a semi-famous copywriter, suddenly down and out on Madison Avenue, the victim of account losses, suddenly thrust into an agency of lesser stature, unhappy and reeling from the shift. I was prime for that significant something.

My own particular passkey to the '80s has been fantasy. I relied on it to get me through the terrorism headlines, the AIDS crisis, the MTV craze or anything else 'of the '80s'. After I hung up on the call, I slipped into my fantasy full-tilt. Andy Warhol wants to meet someone in advertising. This means he will be drawn to my charm and taken by my wit. He will instantly insist that I be part of his cult. Maybe make me his own in-house agency for whatever he wished to promote. Or, grander still, I would finally make that long-awaited advertising leap. I would work on Interview Magazine and run the entire operation. Star in his new films. Be the Edie Sedgwick/Joe Dellasandro 20 years later. Today's Rocky Road to his '60s Cherry Vanilla.

The day of the date, I wondered how to dress for the occasion. Dinner was at eight. I would go home from work and change. That particular day, I was wearing my advertising chic—a sort of Don Johnson meets Mr. Rogers look. From my desk, I mentally went over my closet and realized nothing there would do. Maybe I should run a little black liner around my eyes, look like a haunted writer, with a perpetual cigarette dangling. I decided to call up a friend who met Andy once and ask her advice.

"Andy's a health freak. No drugs. No booze. No caffeine," she said.

Out went the cigarettes. And I figured what I was wearing that day, an argyle vest and a pale pink shirt, was as good as anything.

Dinner was at a place called Caffe Roma, still one more overpriced spaghetti joint in the Positano/Canastel's/La Collona region of New York. That rediscovered area of town once home to photographer's studios and trimming supplies, now taken over by the young, the rich and the restless. I'm there at five of eight, unfashionably early.

A dark-eyed man was leaning on the maître d' podium. I told him I was part of the Warhol party and he told me he wasn't the maître d' but a maître d' over at the River Café in Brooklyn and that he was waiting for his blind date. I wondered if we were both Andy's blind date or were we part of a group. I never liked groups. I always believed I was at my sincere best one on one.

The actual maître d' came over and said we should wait for the rest of the people to arrive—damnit, we were to be a party. Not at all what I pictured. I tense up at the notion of meeting lots of new people all at once, but try to hold onto positive just the same.

Unfashionably on time, Andy arrives and a moment or two later, while I start formulating in my head my pop personality, the rest of the group gathers and we are all led to a series of five tables for two pushed together in front of a banquette against a wall. Five blind dates all at once.

A young, plain woman named Page, Andy's assistant, had a seating plan. You there, you there, you at the end. Introductions were made and names quickly forgotten over handshakes and awkward smiles. In addition to the nervous maître d' seated to my right, there was: a producer for the Letterman show, a young movie star with a '50s cleavage and elbow length black gloves that someone whispered was famous for her work in "The Flamingo Kid," a fairly known clothing designer who had a double page spread running in the current Interview, and a writer named Tama, part of Andy's vague new troupe who looked the part with her dyed black piled-up hair and her dirty fingernails. And then there was the caller, Mr. Greenberg, with a Ben Franklin hairstyle and who was, I came to learn, someone with an investment finger in every pot in town. The two or three others down the table I never did get to meet formally.

We were five blind dates with no common ground, no connections to each other with the exception of Andy's bookended women—his assistant and his aspirant. Other than that and Greenberg, there was no link to any of us, well, perhaps that's what a blind date is all about.

We were as young as 25. As old as Andy. I was somewhere in the middle.

During the first few minutes, after the drinks were ordered (Page ordered pots of water for the herbal tea they brought with them; I ordered a glass of red wine) I raced through all the things in my head that would make me come off witty and interesting, but proceeded to say the most idiotic things. "What's it like to be famous, recognized all the time?" "Is Warren Beatty really doing a movie about you starring Jack Nicholson, the way Page Six reported?" "Do you miss the Factory Underground days?" all blurted out like I was conducting an interview, causing a barrier to rise up between Andy and me like an oversized menu. He was polite enough, kind of shy, but he seemed removed from it all. He was like an observer at the next table, watching all of us and yet somehow manipulating it all.

I turned to the one person I thought I could relate to: the River Café man named Nicky. I asked him how he thought it was going so far and he said he was enjoying himself. I asked him if he thought we were being used somehow, for some reason yet unclear. He told me to relax and enjoy myself.

I wasn't sure how to relax, exactly, so I ordered another glass of wine. This was still my one big chance. If I appeared relaxed and laid back, he's find me boring. At best, I had a few hours or so to be captivating. To change my life.

I felt the pressure of time tick by. Inside of ten minutes, I was confused and lost all sense of how to come off. Clearly, my initial enthusiasm wasn't working. My innocent questions were greeted as if I was taking liberties, like I'd be using his answers in some magazine piece. If I was quiet for a minute or two, I felt I lost him and, with it, my opportunity.

Inside of fifteen minutes, the time he said everyone should be famous for, I saw my fantasies start to fade. Andy seemed no more interested in me or in advertising than he was on most of the items on the menu. But I was determined to hold onto a little of the dream and try to be light.

Politely, he asked me about my watch. That led to all sorts of ramblings about my watch collection, an unfinished watch book I was unsuccessfully peddling, and the book I wrote on diets and all the things I had yet to write.

"Oh, really?" he said. He said 'oh, really' a lot, generally with the same inflection. To his assistant, to the waiter describing a sauce, to the air.

The salads arrive. This prompts Page to whisk out a Sony 8mm cassette camera from her bag and photograph the dishes. With sound. To my mind, there isn't anything particularly photogenic about a salad to inspire moving pictures, even if this one had radicchio of a pretty shade of purple. After a while, Page may have thought so too, because she turned the camera away from the plates and onto the people. Slowly, she surveyed the guests with her Sony, then tucked it away, back in her bag as quickly as she retrieved it.

Andy and I were quiet. The noise from the other diners was enough to fill our void. By the time my spinach-filled ravioli arrived, Page had switched to a still camera with an annoying flash. I had just about given up on Andy by now and, determined to have a conversation, turned to Nicky. He asked if I still felt uncomfortable and I said yes and that now I had the distinct feeling that we were being ridiculed. As I went on, I found him growing more uncomfortable about why he was there. He started smoking Tama's exotic cigarettes and said he hadn't had a cigarette in twenty years.

No job offers, no catapult to stardom, no overnight transformation, not even any parmesan on the ravioli, I head for Mr. Greenberg, our host.

"What's the point of all this?" I ask.

"No point. Just people meeting each other," he said. He admitted the table arrangement was not the best for ten strangers and I wondered how much easier it would have been if we were just a party in a room together, the ten of us, and decided it would have been equally awkward.

Andy had spaghetti with basil and pomodoro because Page said she knew he would like it. Page had swordfish and more pots of hot water. She was distressed to learn there was no fresh fruit on the dessert menu, but the manager arranged for some to arrive, no doubt orange slices and strawberries used by the bartender as garnish, hastily arranged to give the restaurant a favorable nod from this important client. And there were other important people afoot: Oleg Cassini was seated right behind me with some tennis pro and two women with Kathleen Turner hairdos. Pauline Trigére was at another table, filled with people, that turned into a birthday celebration. The place was packed for a Monday night in New York. Young people kept walking in well past eleven, stopping to notice Andy, convinced that finally, they were in the right place at the right time.

With the ice helplessly unbroken, a birthday cake arrives and is placed in front of Tama. She's surprised and embarrassed, then delighted with herself for being able to blow out both candles with a single breath. I tell her it's my birthday, too. Well, on Sunday. Andy says: "Oh, really?"

Though the check was already paid by Page, the waiters passed around champagne glasses and poured Moët from bottle after bottle. The crowd was now loose, but still uncomfortable. I was having a horrible time and longed for my bed, my VCR, my thousandth viewing of "All About Eve," but I stayed firm in my chair, hoping now against hope, that this thing was to finally get off the ground and something would become clear.

A hostess came over to me and said I had a phone call.

I knew it had to be the friend I told this 'life-changing dinner' and when it was her, she said I should go back to the table and say it was something about last script changes that I had to okay, to make them feel like I was terribly important, but when I came back to the table, it appeared that no one noticed that I was gone or that I was back. Not even Nicky.

Pauline Trigére, apparently realizing that Andy wasn't going to get up and come over to her table after all, deemed herself to approach our table and say hello to Andy over my shoulder, extending a limp, ringed hand. She looked fabulous, I thought, for her age, all stylish with her cardboard hair and her signature glasses. I told her, too. "You look fabulous," I said, beaming and sincere, and she looked down at me like I was small and unimportant. I decided she didn't look all that good up close.

From then on, I knew I had had it. My afternoon dreams were as shriveled as a day-old basil leaf. I decided to take myself out of there before I had one more glass of champagne and say something really stupid that no one would have heard, anyway.

As it happened, everyone decided it was time to leave after all. The party that never really started, had ended. Coats were retrieved, goodbyes were said, and Page told me to have a safe trip back to Princeton. It was Nicky who was on his way to Princeton. Page, in her herbal tea stupor, had gotten us confused.

I shook Andy's white hand and said goodbye. "Maybe I'll see you again," I venture. "That would be nice," he said. I think he meant to say: "Oh, really?"

In the cab home, depressed and half-drunk, it dawned on me. The point. The reason. It wasn't that all blind dates are disastrous no matter how rich or how famous or how low cut the bodice. It was a phone call that changed my life, somewhat. I always thought how wonderful it would be to be rich and famous and then, in the cab, I thought differently. I mean, if Andy Warhol has to arrange to have dinner with perfect strangers and pay for it all himself, what good is it to be well-known and recognized? He's undoubtedly just as bored as you and I. And probably more so.

— 1986

What's a Supermodel To Do?

If you're worried that you're out of work, consider the plight of Christie Brinkley. OK, she's married to a man that no doubt gets big, fat royalty checks every day in the mail. We're talking Mrs. Billy Joel here. Pretty, famous, venture to say one of the original supermodels. Christie. This is about her life and her future.

Last Thursday, I overheard her talking to her husband and an unknown third party over lunch at East Hampton's Maidstone Arms. She was wondering where she was headed. What she could possibly do next now that her modeling career seemed stalled. I could relate to that, finding the next thing, having just finished up a nine-month freelance stint in advertising, wondering where I was headed. In that time, I wrote a campaign for M&M's,

a new worldwide tagline and a bunch of commercials, but it was suddenly over. For me, that achievement—fleeting, meaningless, was somehow comparable to her last on-the-air debacle, her fast defunct cable series: *Living in the 90's with Christie Brinkley*.

The '90s.

As I sat with my poached chicken and mashed potatoes, watching her, then pretending not to watch her, I suspected she wished it were still the '80s. Christie was very famous in the '80s. And thinner. Sitting there, concerned, she looked slightly fuller in the face. She seemed to have a hint of an additional chin, heck, it was more than a hint, it was practically a whole other chin! Yet she was pretty, even if there was a bit more of her.

She ordered the weakfish, dressing on the side, and told her husband that she kept wishing her metabolism would kick back in, wondering if it ever would. I guessed she was currently somewhere in her mid to late 30s, the age when metabolisms start doing exactly as they damned well please, thank you very much.

Billy Joel, at about 45, seemed unconcerned and rather comfortable with his weight, spilling over the sides of the antique dining chair. He had some chins as well, the first one wrapped in a beard. Thankfully, my frontal view was of Christie with her long hair and her perfectly done face. A beautiful face, but with a definite look of concern,

What's a Supermodel To Do?

wondering what great thing could she possibly do next.

Like all of us, I know plenty of unknowns, smaller in their success than Christie Brinkley perhaps, but just as out of work as she is and not so young anymore as she is, looking for their value in this pared-down life in the '90s. I also know plenty of nobodies who are still working but still wondering when they will be laid off, what will become of them, and where will they be going from here.

After they ordered, a frizzy-haired woman joined them, resting her thick Filofax by her plate. She had a job, I was sure of that, working for them. She had that harried job attitude about her, rushed and flustered. Whoever she was, she was no one important enough for Christie and Billy to wait to order. Ms. Frizz ordered a Diet Coke and settled right into the topic at hand: Where does Christie go from here?

What made overhearing this conversation for me very interesting was that some years before, in 1984, I had two dinners with Ms. Brinkley to discuss her ideas developing a swimsuit line. A line designed by her. An art director friend (let's call her Rochelle, because her name was Rochelle) and I were to come up with ideas for its television commercial introduction. Christie was beautiful in 1984, with clear, sparkly blue eyes. Nine years ago, at those dinners, she ordered Dom Pérignon. Today, she ordered one decaf cappuccino after another and a large Ty Nant water, sparkling. Christie was hot in 1984. She was fresh from Cover Girl and

Back in the Star Again

from the original girlie covers of Sports Illustrated's illustrious swimsuit issues. She was engaged to Billy at the time, whom she referred to as "Joe" between coy sips of DP as she described her shallow ideas for the swimwear.

We created a campaign, Rochelle and I, something that seems frivolous to me now, but it didn't much matter. The advertising was never produced. The swimsuit line sank like a stone in a matter of months.

"Paris. We'll live in Paris, or Rome. Of course, it would have to be a city," Billy said as his cheeseburger arrived.

"I've lived in Paris," Christie said, bored. That wouldn't do. She wanted a job, not a city.

I ordered an espresso. Billy had two quick red wines. I like that he had wine during the day—this was a gray, cool May day, perfect for a dulling afternoon buzz. Maybe he would go back to his Amagansett beachfront and write a new standard ballad about the future of all of us out-of-workers: "Just The Way You Wish You Were," perhaps. Meantime, he talked about other supermodels of the past—Veruschka and Jean Shrimpton. Twiggy, Cheryl Tiegs and Lauren Hutton. He didn't mention Claudia Schiffer or Linda Evangelista or Christy Turlington. Cindy Crawford's name didn't come out of his mouth. He mentioned a Kelly and a Kim, but he couldn't remember their last names. He described them as Christie look-alikes, that distinctive, blond, California look and with that same uptown girl attitude. I knew he was referring to Kelly Emberg and Kim Alexis. But, clearly, he didn't want to talk about the girls that came after Christie. In her dark mood of uncertainty, he didn't want to upset her with talk of the new and now modeling world. I thought: what a considerate husband.

He also talked a lot of ideas, possibilities, things she could align herself to popped out of him like succinct lyrics. He said that fragrance was out and Dickinson's Witch Hazel was in, and Pinaud for Men was back and great, that turquoise liquid from the barber shops of his youth, when he had a full head of hair. That's what people wanted today. Maybe she could just tap into this natural phenomenon? People want natural, that's what's new, he said. I thought: sure, as new as granola or Euell Gibbons, or bell bottoms. Everything old is new again, yet Christie seemed unmoved by the suggestions as she picked at her plain, pale plate of fish.

Well, at least everyone was talking about her—that was something nice. Still, she looked concerned. What is to become of a model? Even one of the original supermodels who's staring down 40? Her frizzy-haired friend, the lady who had to order later (but they're clever at the Maidstone, the waitress brought all the food out at once), said infomercials were big and QVC was hot and MTV still untapped. She was talking about the future, the next big thing and wondering how she could capitalize further on this beautiful model, turning ever so slightly to fat, hoping for a few more good years, the frizzy-haired woman herself hoping for a few more good years, myself hoping for a few more good years, so many of us hoping for a few more good years.

My check came. I wondered if I should go over and sit in the fourth chair at their table. I wondered if I should say to Christie: hey, remember me—I'm the guy that helped you with that swimsuit line that lasted a season? Like *Living in the 90's with Christie Brinkley*, a season. For a minute, I fantasized like the frizzy-haired friend, why not? I could shape Christie's future. Make life work for her beyond the '90s, into the '00s and beyond. But I felt cowardly and like no one they would care to know, so I paid the check, sipped the last gritty remains of my coffee, and thought: I have my own problems finding work.

When I left the restaurant and walked out into the East Hampton spring mist, I thought no matter how rich, no matter how famous, how old or how young, everyone wonders where they are going from here. I thought no matter what we have earned or saved or how much we owe, what we may have achieved or hope to achieve or fantasize about achieving, everyone wonders what's going to happen next. Christie, honey, good luck to you. And to all of us.

— 1993

South of Highway Robbery

We share a nice house in the Amagansett dunes, my friend David and I. Nothing too elaborate, at least not by the standards one sees out here. We had two televisions in this house, two VCRs, a random compact disc player, a cassette deck and receiver, all Sonys. There were Bose speakers—an indulgence at slightly under a thousand dollars, but they looked great and worked really well.

Monday night, October 25, 1992, we wuz robbed.

They made out like bandits. And with our clothes, too. They took some sports jackets and a suit: Armanis and Hugo Boss; clothing they wouldn't have gotten a week from now. We would have moved them back to New York, the winter-weights. But they would have gotten the seersuckers and the lightweight Calvin Kleins.

Back in the Star Again

We switch closets, as it were, twice a year. We both like (liked) our clothing on the boxy side. So, East Hampton police, take note: The perps could be anywhere from five-seven to six-one, between 150 and 210 pounds, and still wearing these clothes well.

A down jacket with a pink triangle pin attached to the collar was taken.

A suede baseball jacket, red with black sleeves, also is gone. And good riddance, they can have that tired old number, though I would have rather tossed it, with other dated yet highly wearable items, in the donating bin for the Order of St. Vincent de Paul that sits in the A&P parking lot on Newtown Lane.

There are plenty of CDs gone. The whole collection, actually, that sat in a now-wrecked antique pie cabinet, painted a washed-out acid green. Elton John, gone. Billy Joel, poof. Anita Baker, missing. They left behind, as if in giddy afterthought, Streisand's four-CD set swathed in pink, "Just for the Record," and Marlene Dietrich's "Dietrich in Rio." It's a good guess these crooks were not gay.

David discovered the theft on a gray Tuesday afternoon, between the Film Festival and Halloween. The day before, the house watcher had come inside to check on the house as he'd done every Monday and Thursday for the last twelve years and always with nothing out of the ordinary to report. But Tuesday at 4:00, when David arrived from

New York with the dogs, the place was a disaster.

   Shaky, he called the police, then called me, back in New York, and left a message on my voice mail, as calm and controlled as he could. When I reached him back, he blurted out all the damage he had so far assessed while the policemen were there, dusting for prints.

   All those electronics. Even a telephone, the new black Sony. They left the yellow Princess phone behind, damn. If they had to take a phone, I would rather they had taken the Princess and not the Sony, but I suppose they, too, realize how difficult it is to get a bank balance from a rotary phone, no matter how campy.

   It's a minimum two and a half hours from there to here, on a good day, so I had all that time to imagine what all else they might have taken.

   I was sure they'd found the spare Mercedes key, on a ring with a chunky gold-toned Mercedes logo (a gift from the dealer, I'm not that tacky). The spare in the sock drawer! They took it and they'd be back to get the car, I was convinced.

   They ripped off the Philippe Starck-ish door handles. Two of them, frosted turquoise and amber resin jobbies in a wave pattern, a find in Paris during Christmas '91. And, oh, Christ, they took the rayon baseball cap in that '50s drapery pattern I cherish so, a birthday gift that I really look good in.

   What they did take was a signed Irving Penn photo

book, but they left the new Richard Avedon autobiography (unsigned). What? They're partial to pictures of leaves and not people?

The cops dusted a large, soft-covered Bruce Weber book, also signed. It's not ruined, exactly, but it's deeply embedded with black fingerprint dust, casting a grayish haze on the cover photo of Bruce's young and vacant Rio de Janeiroans. I understand Bruce likes his books somewhat distressed; it shows they've been looked at.

When I entered the house, exactly two and a half hours later, no traffic, just your basic lane-closed kind of LIE, David had had enough time to get over the fear that the thieves were still lurking somewhere with our eight-inch Sabatier, and enough time to clear up the heavy evidence that the place had been ransacked.

First thing he told me was a pair of black shoes, suede lace-ups size 11C, were right there by the bedroom chair as if someone had tried them on. There was mildew on the shoes. If you live near the ocean you know what havoc that can do to suede shoes in closets. The creeps decided against these.

Perhaps they were too large, or else too moldy, though that residue is easily removable with a suede brush, which I guess he didn't notice was sitting right there on the shelf next to the Gianni Versace cologne they were so grateful to come by.

I am your basic, run-of-the-mill neurotic Jew, like I don't

have enough genetic disturbances. I am prone to hysteria from the littlest thing. Miraculously, arriving at the scene of the crime, I was calm.

I had a pack of cigarettes, my first in two years. I had bought the pack after a rock or something equally hostile smacked itself into the windshield of my two-month-old Mercedes, at Exit 69 on my way out. (It's not what you think with the Mercedes. It's the mini-Mercedes and with that win-win lease, I got the thing for less a month than I was paying for the boomer-ish Saab 900 when that lease expired.)

I figured, after the windshield got smacked and cracked, I was entitled to a couple of Marlboro Lights. I actually had the whole pack in the next 24 hours, while the house was getting back to normal, well a normal deprived of roughly $12,000 worth of stuff. Just stuff, I tried to tell myself, and maybe I heard David muttering that too. Just stuff. Stuff can be replaced.

We slept. It rained overnight. I had some trouble sleeping at first. Thinking about all the stuff. Though they took off with a vintage Cartier watch and a Nikon and a Polaroid. (Where and when and why did we get all these things?)

I kept trying to remember which CDs it was exactly that they took, we being of the two-home CD collection variety. I wondered at 2:00 a.m.: Was the *Billboard Top Disco Hits of 1978* gone? The Natalie Cole *Unforgettable*? The *Paris*

Back in the Star Again

By Night? The things you think of when you're robbed and can't sleep…sleep…

The next morning it was still raining, but, somehow, gloriously. The colors of the leaves were so beautiful they were almost painful to look at. We drove to the police station to have ourselves fingerprinted—"elimination prints," they called them.

We often drive from Beach Hampton to East Hampton via Further Lane, passing by the golf course and the pond, that stretch of perfection that never diminishes in any light, even with the reality of our morning after.

We drove through a flock of scattering blackbirds; vivid against the flame orange of a group of trees, staggering in the slowly emerging sunlight. We got ourselves fingerprinted to distinguish our prints from the burglars', that is, if they weren't wearing gloves. At least they didn't get any gloves from us, not even my faux beaver mitts from Bergdorf Men's safely nestled behind three locks, a handful of doormen, and elevator guys in the blissful safety of Manhattan.

After the prints, I called my insurance company, an East Hampton carrier, and told the nice agent the news. I didn't feel that I had been ravaged, particularly. Or violated or raped like some people say after they've been broken into.

On hold with the insurance company, I looked around the house. They didn't take the walls. They didn't make off with the views from the large plate-glass second-story windows, views that look up at any number of Long Island skies in all colors from powder blue to chartreuse to pale pink purple.

They didn't take the starry black nights. They didn't take the afghan my mother hand-knitted. It was there, just like before, slung over a simple couch. They didn't take the love in the rooms. They didn't take the dogs. All that was still there, so screw you, robbers!

They came in through the living room window, a window hidden by shrubbery. A window I paid good money for to block off the house from the quiet road, empty as a potato field in October. The cops, while we were being fingerprinted, said it's something how people pay to have their house made so private from the road, only to have it come back and bite them in the *tuchas*—because all the overgrown shrubbery makes it possible for a burglar to spend a month prying open a window in the off-season without anyone seeing.

I looked out the window, this particular half-hour's view, blue and gray, serene and severe, the aftermath of a storm as it can only storm out here. The sun was making a strong appearance suddenly, already drying up the huge puddles in the streets of the Dunes, disappearing almost as you watched.

After I hung up from the insurance company, I called my father, a habit, thank the Lord, I'm not out of when things go amiss, even at 45. He's a dear man and someone who has

Back in the Star Again

seen a lot. His immediate response was: You do have all your receipts, right? And: At least they didn't take the dogs.

Freeda and Archie, the terriers, are still with us. Rather than be ripped off Freeda, the wire-haired fox, especially would have put up a stink had she been there. She knows where her comforts lie.

The Marlboro Lights are finished. The Ralph Lauren towels, canary yellow, emerald green, fuschia and others, are gone. Pillowcases, to lug the stuff, gone. The outdoor garbage can, history. The inventory forms from the insurance company are on their way in the mail.

The swans, oblivious to our or anyone else's plight this October day, dipped their heads in that pond fringed by those trees as we drove to Caldor to replace the garbage can immediately, the most important thing we needed to replace. Frank Sinatra's *Only the Lonely* CD and something to play it on could definitely wait.

The early afternoon sun was already golden with the promise of a larger sun to come, rounder and more orange than any of those pumpkins that dot the landscape everywhere this day. One look at those swans, the sun, the Maidstone country club with its mystery in the seductive distance, and there is no thought of moving away from the place because of the insanity of the episode.

No thoughts of Litchfield, Connecticut or the Berkshires or Fire Island or anywhere else perhaps more remote where maybe the crooks haven't cracked yet. We lunched, like princes, at the Maidstone Arms, a treat after our ordeal, a treat even when there is no ordeal.

Dyed-in-the-wool Hamptonites, us, scrappy New Yorkers, scrappy as wire-haired fox terriers, suddenly find ourselves invulnerable, ultimately, and unflappable by uncontrollable forces. We wonder, as we decide between Dinkins and Giuliani, between Amagansett and nowhere, if there really is an answer or a respite between reality and utopia.

If there is indeed a place to feel really safe now, to say nothing of our job statuses, or does safety really and only have to do with love and dogs (or children) and what's inside of us? Not accoutrements inside a house. We wonder.

There was one piece of electronic equipment they didn't get, because we didn't have it. A security system, an alarm with a siren and a keypad and magnetic charges generating currents between doors and jambs and windows and panes. And motion sensors. We didn't have a security system. But one is being installed as you read.

We love to hate the Hamptons. But also, we love to love them, baby.

Damn! Donna Summer's three-disc anthology is gone, too.

— 1993

Renée and Me

I don't gush much. It takes a certain amount to impress me.

The last serious movie star crush I had was on Sandra Dee back in the '60s but that was a high school thing.

Yes, I do read People and I sometimes see Page Six, but I'm not a star fucker, per se. This is about fate. And Renée Zellweger and me.

As backstory, you should know my female favorites from the movies. I very much like Shirley MacLaine in *The Apartment*. (Renée sometimes reminds me of Shirley.) I love *All About Eve* and *Whatever Happened to Baby Jane* and also *Now, Voyager*. My mother was a huge fan of Bette Davis. I agree she was a great actress too, but a little before my time, so she's harder to call your own when you can only see her on old videos and DVDs. Meryl is really good. Glenn Close, I like. Also Doris Day for a while.

But it's Renée Zellweger that is it for me, and the reason is because I have a connection to her in a way that I never did with any other movie star. You see, I run into her all the time. The first time I saw her was during her thirtieth birthday celebration at a restaurant called Barefoot in Los Angeles. I was alone at a table having lunch and nearby was a large group of blond people with Southern accents. I was writing while I was eating but I couldn't help but overhear. Turns out it was Renée and her family, all up from Texas, celebrating her big birthday. I got the sense that it was a weekend long party; this was the brunch part of it. I recognized Renée, but at that time wasn't particularly interested in her. It was post *Jerry Maguire*, pre *Bridget Jones*. It could have been her *Me, Myself & Irene* moment. Or maybe around the time of *One True Thing* (with the aforementioned Meryl). I almost felt like an invited guest at the brunch. Though I was at the next table, I heard all they were talking about: family stuff, life in Texas, sweet reminiscences. I was drawn to her, suddenly. She seemed sweet. Unpretentious.

I live in New York and occasionally see stars. I saw Julia Roberts once on lower Fifth. Warren Beatty and Annette Bening on upper Madison one sunny Saturday. Random spottings. One time only.

I also travel to Los Angeles often for business reasons.

Back in the Star Again

So I see stars there too. Sean Penn at the Four Seasons. Mark Wahlberg. Morgan Freeman and Jeff Daniels once together in the same elevator. I did see Rosie O'Donnell twice, once at Joe Allen in New York and again, also in the Four Seasons Hotel elevator. But I run into Renée Zellweger all the time. I mean, all the time.

The second time I saw her up close was when she was a more substantial star. I was at Lucques, a hot restaurant in LA at the time, 2001 or so. There were other stars there that night—Robert De Niro, Julia Louis-Dreyfus. And then Renée walked in in a strapless dress and sat right at De Niro's table! A new movie deal together?! The three of them!? There was a big buzz about it all in the restaurant, paparazzi hovered outside, and then, she was off in a car. And it was over.

Some months later, back in LA, I saw her again. But this was more than just a casual spotting. We actually got to speak. It was at another restaurant, The Little Door. I was there with a small group, and Liz, a coworker, had to go to the ladies' room. I escorted her there as I had to go to the men's room. The men's was locked, the women's, free. Liz went in and I stood there, waiting. And then, this blonde woman appears. Walks briskly over to the ladies' room door and yanks on the handle. "Hold on," I say. "My friend is in there." Then I realize it's her. "Oh. Hi," I say. "You're Renée Zellweger."

She said, yes, she was. She was wearing a sky blue satin dress with spaghetti straps. It was at this precise moment that I felt we were destined to meet. I gushed, well, I don't gush much, but I felt I knew her. "I really like your work," I said, trying to sound Hollywood. That's what they say in Hollywood about roles. They say work.

Liz took awhile in the ladies. "I saw you in *Nurse Betty*. You're great," I said. I meant it. It helps to be sincere when you address celebrities. They can pretty much tell the difference.

Needless to say by now, I felt like I knew her. And I felt like she knew me. Although I was just a fan, smitten more and more as I watched her and spoke to her at a bunch of restaurants now, I thought she would recognize and know me too. I felt we were fated. I mean, now it's three times I've seen her. And I don't live in LA. We chatted like friends, casually. I told her I had seen her before but was careful to not come off as a stalker. She smiled her smile. She tilted her head to the side like she does, pursing her lips, squinting, nodding. Liz exited the bathroom.

"Oh, Liz, this is my friend, Renée," I said. "Renée, Liz."

Liz has some semi-celebrity friends so she was not so struck by the meeting. I thought it was cool, though. I mean, how often does a nobody get to introduce Renée Zellweger to somebody?

The Golden Globes happened a month or two after

Back in the Star Again

The Little Door bathroom event. Renée won something—for *Nurse Betty*, I think. It was before *Bridget Jones*. Before *Chicago*. She accepted the award, pursing, smiling, tilting, squinting, and I thought, for one crazy second as you do if you're crazy, that she would make some reference to me. "Here's to the salt-and-pepper haired man I met outside the washrooms at The Little Door. To the guy writing by himself at Barefoot. To the guy checking me out at Lucques."

Nope. I was not referenced.

Today I read she got her marriage annulled. Friends of mine who have endured my fascination with Renée, my adoration, this connection, called me, all day long, to let me know. But I knew already. The same night of the day she was single again, I went to The Palm in East Hampton for dinner with my friend David. As we were finishing, he said to me: Don't turn around, but outside there, on the cell phone, is Renée Zellweger. David knows full well how I feel about her—he was the first one to tell me this morning's news of her breakup.

Fate, I thought. I have to talk to her, I told David. And I left the table and went out to the bench, outside the restaurant, where she was sitting, talking on the phone. I waited. She finished her call. "It's me, Hy," I said. "Do you remember me?"

(As it happens, by some other fateful coincidence, a friend of mine, Steven, is decorating her New York rental apartment and her newly purchased home in Connecticut. Her house in East Hampton is barely a mile from my place in Amagansett. I mean, really, isn't there some important connection going on here?)

"I don't remember you, sorry," she said at The Palm, coyly, very Renée-ey, tilting, smiling, pursing, squinting. "I meet so many people."

"I was right there, at your thirtieth," I said. Almost like an invited guest.

"And there, at The Little Door, You were waiting to get into the ladies' room. I introduced you to Liz," I continued.

"I loved you in *Chicago*. You were amazing in *Cold Mountain*."

David came out to join us. "It's true," he said. "This here is your biggest fan."

"Will you remember me the next time we run into each other? My name is Hy," I said, sure we would see each other again and again, New York, Connecticut, West Hollywood, East Hampton. I mean, really, wouldn't you say our lives are intertwined?

I never met Sandra Dee (and never will). I guess I could see Shirley MacLaine at the Four Seasons—even after she's dead. Bette Davis I will only see again and again in black and white as Margo Channing. But I know for sure that I will run into Renée Zellweger forever, until the day we both die.

It's kind of karmic, don't you think? Today, she's all over

the news with her failed marriage. And there I was, in my own way, there for her as I will be there for her, the only movie star in my universe that I will ever have this kind of connection with.

I don't gush much. But, really, wouldn't you if this had happened to you?

— 2005

Forgiveness, Hampton Style

I have a peanut pool. That's what my pool guy calls it. It's teeny-tiny.

That pool guy fired me today in a fit of craziness. He admits to being crazy. I have been known to be same.

This is a story of forgiveness. Of getting past things. Past tempers and anger and craziness.

My teeny-tiny peanut pool got blotchy. Concrete pools get blotchy, I had heard, because the hockey-puck chemicals pool guys plop in pools are so powerful. Powerful enough to cause burns, holes in the concrete! Circular burns that turn a pool blotchy.

"Marble-dusting gets the pool back to new. Banishes the blotchiness," my pool-guy said. "Your pool is due for a dusting."

I had to admit, it was due. A friend of mine, Sam, a photographer, took a picture last year of the pool that hangs, framed, in the kitchen. And you can see in the photo how blotchy the pool precisely is.

"Bring on the dusting," I say, a believer in beach house maintenance.

I agree to the dusting in January. Pool guy says he will get in touch with the guy who does the dusting and will get back to me. "Best to do it before we open," he says. "I'll get back to you in a few weeks."

We are not there in the winter. The water is shut off, the house hibernates, awaiting our return in early April.

Flash forward to late March. Pool guy seemed also to be hibernating, him and his workers. I wonder (and don't) why I haven't heard back as months from the decision to dust has passed.

"Hey, pool guy," I call, end of March. "Whatever happened to the marble duster?"

"What a coinckidinki!" he says. "The guy that does the dusting just called today! And he's ready to do the job. Today! Only thing is—is your outside water turned on?"

I'm surprised by the coincidence, surprised and suspicious. But I'm glad it's to be done. "I'll have to check with my house watcher about the water," I say. (I think: it's months since we've determined the dusting would be done. All of a sudden, it's today.)

Forgiveness, Hampton Style

As my old, dear friend Sandy Goebel had said, in response to my frustration over the workers here on the East End: If they wanted to be more successful, they'd be in New York. Read: They're out surfing, or drinking, relieved to be free of the New York people with their outrageous demands, they secretly object to us, pushy and demanding and RIGHT THIS MINUTE. Well, now, that shoe was on the other foot: RIGHT THIS MINUTE is when the duster was ready to dust.

You should know, I dread calling my house watcher. Though dependable and sweet as can be, he never returns my calls. Thing is, he does what I ask him to do on the message, but never lets me know it's been done until I get to the house and see it's been taken care of. He doesn't call back, but he has a beeper, which I'm reluctant to use. Nothing seems like enough of an emergency. You have only twelve seconds to leave your message on the beeper, another thing that unnerves me—I never know if I can get all the information out in those miniscule seconds. But I do the beeper because the pool guy seemed so insistent I find out about the water. RIGHT THIS MINUTE! So I beep him and he calls right back.

"I would strongly recommend against turning on the water at this juncture," house watcher says. "One last cold snap…" and then the connection goes to the 'Can you hear me now?' variety. I'm in an elevator, rushing to my office when this conversation—"What was that? Are you there?" takes place. "Hello?" I screech, conscious of the imminent disconnection. "Hello? Hello?" Nothing. Then the elevator doors open and I get off on the cafeteria floor, calling back the house watcher, getting his machine, calling the beeper again. And we reconnect: "I strongly recommend against turning on the outside water until April 10th."

From the cafeteria, now late for a meeting, and annoyed, very annoyed, that all this stuff, this back and forth, has to happen in a minute (RIGHT THIS MINUTE!) after months of waiting. Now here's where the story gets really crazy.

Cell phone to cell phone. Me to pool guy: "My house watcher strongly recommends I do not turn the outside water on," I say, gesticulating, crazed in the cafeteria.

"But it's today. IT'S TODAY! (Like a Jerry Herman lyric.) We have him today and he's ready to do the dusting!"

Now, I'm over the edge. I get there quick, you should know. Redemptionally, I get over it just as quick.

"You expletive mean that after all these expletive months of nothing, it's this expletive minute or never?" The question should be in all caps. Seconds it took to say this, but it caused a reaction in pool guy that I didn't quite expect.

"I'm sorry. I am. Sorry. Sorry to have ruined your day. So sorry. I can no longer be your pool guy."

"What? Isn't that a little extreme?" I ask, already calming down and kind of in shock. I wondered just how angry my being angry is. I wondered just how crazy was this pool guy. Was I actually being fired by the pool guy?

He hangs up. No dropped connection there, a clear, sharp hang up. I stand there, in the cafeteria, numb, shocked, shaking. Guilty, some. My anger, like Naomi Campbell's, at times, I must confess, has caused this larger than life reaction. Fired by the pool guy? In an instant?? His own anger, his own pride or something telling him that the $300 or so he gets to plop fizzy chemical hockey pucks in my teeny-tiny peanut pool four times a month, a job easy as pie, was not worth it to him if he has to confront a crazy like me?

Dropped by him, freaked by his reaction, I leave the cafeteria and run into my assistant and blurt out the whole shocking story. "Do I strike you as an angry guy, Lindsay?" I ask, shaken, my fingernails at my mouth, anxious.

"You? I don't see it," she says. Good girl. Knowing what to say. Political in a corporate environment. But still, I did, then and there, question my own correctness. So much anger as a result of so much anger. Does anger beget anger? I guess it must. This episode, fired by my pool guy, forced me to examine my own history of explosiveness. Of course, it takes two to tango—or do much of anything else, but being fired by the pool guy, relating the incident to my sweet assistant, a 22-year old person who I'd never seen lose her temper or doubt never had a temper lost against her, gave me pause to reevaluate and wonder how much blame to take. All? Half? None? I needed to figure it out.

"It's probably best that you don't talk about this too much just now. Wait an hour or two," Lindsay says, wise beyond her years. She saw how shocked and shaken I was.

I knew she was talking about David, my partner of 21 years who judges and looks askance at my tendency towards tirades. David, dear David, who often takes the side of the person on the other end, just to keep me in check and tow. How to explain this to him? That we were dropped, unceremoniously, in an instant, by the pool person. David, who has gotten me out of my scrappy scraps one too many times over the years. It was good advice from Lindsay, but as soon as I got back to my desk, my phone was ringing. Caller ID: David.

Impulsively, I reach for the receiver, not heeding Lindsay's advice. I quickly blurt out what happened.

"It wasn't my fault..." I say. "The guy's a nut job."

Of course, David was: a) alarmed b) upset c) frustrated and d) all of the above.

"I'll handle it," I say. "I'll find us another pool guy. There are thousands of them listed in the Star." (Even though it's David who usually has the job of handling these things.)

I hang up. Call directory assistance. There are hundreds of pool guys out there. "Get me the number of Tortorella! And John Rachel! And Pelican Pools!" Hundreds.

Just then, my cell phone rings. My ex-pool guy!

"I don't know how to tell you this, Hy," he starts. "But

the marble-dusting has been done. The guy borrowed your neighbor's hose and did the job just this morning. Without me officially authorizing it. Without you officially approving it."

"Huh?"

"I'm paying for it," he continues. "I'm on my way to a cash machine to pay him."

I didn't know what to say.

"Now, here's what you and your new pool guy are gonna hafta do," he goes on. "He's got to stir it up, has to vacuum daily, has to make sure the filter is on 24 hours a day for the next two weeks."

I scramble to write it all down, unsure, crazy, quiet.

"The pool looks brand new, by the way," ex-pool guy says.

I hang up and call David. "You won't believe the turn this all has taken," I say and tell him the turn it has taken.

"I'm calling him. You're just going to have to bite the bullet because I'm going to ask him to be our pool guy again," David says.

I hang up and sit still. And think hard about it. I had been taken to tsk-ey task. I had been fired. I decide, then and there, to forgive. That decision in a flash of…what? turning 60? Feeling anger never got me nowhere? In a flash of clear knowing, I am changed. Changed, I think, forever, although forever is a long time and it is certainly too soon to tell.

David calls back and says he told the once-then-ex-now-reinstated pool guy that Hy insists we both forget about this morning's craziness and get on with moving on. Towards forgiveness. I am pleased. Secretly, privately pleased.

David ends with: "Oh, and I told him to bill us for the dusting."

The following Saturday, us at the house, the once-again pool guy comes over to vacuum and filter and check on the progress. We shake hands. For some reason, I want to hug him, but don't.

"My wife calls it my 911 moment, what happened, when I fired you," he says.

"I've had those," I say, tears welling up in my eyes. "I can be crazy, too."

"Bygones, bygones?" he asks.

"Bygones, bygones," I answer.

It's too soon to tell if this episode will change either of us. Change us from hot heads to cool customers. But it sure felt good to not have to worry that I would run into him at Sam's Pizzeria and have to pretend I don't see him.

We were far from friends, but, in a way, we were something even more surprising:

We were two guys who, finally, did not let their anger get the better of them.

— 2008

My Night With Nora

Nora Ephron is funny. Not hilariously funny, or silly funny, or grossly funny. She's clever funny. Jewish funny. Intellectually funny. Like Woody Allen, or David Sedaris, or Mike Nichols when he was partnered with Elaine May funny.

I have been a fan of Nora Ephron's for decades. I thought *When Harry Met Sally* was very funny and even iconic with that famous Meg Ryan scene, her pretend orgasm and the response from a nearby diner: "I'll have what she's having." Nora Ephron wrote that line and she has her place in history with that alone.

But more obscure (and just as funny) is her collection of 1960s essays: *Wallflower at the Orgy*. And then there was *Sleepless in Seattle, You've Got Mail* then, at a lower point, a Julie Kavner movie I forget the name of that she wrote and directed before Julie Kavner struck it rich as Marge Simpson. Back on the plus side, there's also *Silkwood*, which she wrote the screenplay for, and *Heartburn*, which she wrote as autobiographical novel/cookbook (clever) which became a Mike Nichols movie with Meryl Streep and Jack Nicholson, no less. And then there was, and is: *I Feel Bad About My Neck*, her recent collection of essays about aging. Very funny.

Except, you don't necessarily laugh out loud with Nora Ephron. You laugh inside. Smart. Sophisticated. New York.

I recently went to see a stage reading here in the Hamptons of her new play, adapted from a bestseller that she didn't write. I thought that was generous of her, to adapt at this stage of her career instead of being the control freak most celebrities turn into. She, and her less famous sister, adapted a book and turned it into a play called *Love, Loss and What I Wore*, and they both showed up to answer questions and get feedback about the reading. When I saw an ad for the event in the Star featuring a picture of its star, Linda Lavin, in a new Nora (and Delia) Ephron play, a stage reading at Bridgehampton Community House, I thought: that's for me! Clearly, she's an idol of mine—I aspire to be that kind of clever, heck, I am clever, but I'm not famous like her. My partner, David, doesn't share my cleverness or my idolatry, but I got us two tickets and he went along just the same.

But before we set out to see the show, I went to Book-hampton and bought a couple of her books to be signed, and put something else in that small, yellow, Scoop shopping bag for her, but I won't reveal what that was until the end because it's funny and I want to save that for the ending. Well, it's not hilarious, it's clever and appropriate, so keep reading if you want to find out what it was.

The play was fairly funny. Not hilarious, not silly, not gross, although boobs were mentioned—shopping for bras after a mastectomy (poignant funny). Prom dresses. Wedding dresses. Divorce dresses. What they wore. When they wore it. Who they were with when they wore what they wore. She does this repetitious thing; her humor has a lot to do with things repeated in a rhythm that makes a subtly funny point, over and over. And over.

When it was over, the actors left and the sisters took to the stage. "We know it's not perfect, this is the second time, the second time this is being viewed by people and I, well, *we* want to hear what you think of it," Nora said. Or something, something like that.

The play, as far as this story goes, is beside the point. The point is, there she was, a real Hamptons/NY celebrity! She, who can claim Mike Nichols and Carly Simon as friends (I'm assuming they all met during *Heartburn* which Mike Nichols directed and Carly Simon wrote the songs for) and there I was, with my bag of books and what all else at my feet, my nose pressed up against the window-

Back in the Star Again

pane of celebrity, of writers, of Hamptonites, of B-listers—Kathy Najimy also was part of the stage reading and three other women, lesser stars, nobodies, but not quite as nobody as me, since there they were neck and neck with celebrity. Perhaps, in the end, all celebrities are just like you and me, I guess, but then again, not quite. They are on the best seller list, and they receive residuals from sitcoms, and they have Meryl Streep on speed dial and, although, I'm not Carly Simon, not Paul Simon, I'm not Simple Simon, either. I'm successful enough. I have a very cool beach house practically a Frisbee toss from Sarah Jessica Parker's. I enjoy a long, lucrative career in advertising (see *What I Do* further along in this collection). I work out at Body Tech alongside Liev Schrieber and I've seen Bernadette Peters there once too. And Donny Deutsch a couple of times. But I digress to impress.

The play wore on. The performers were actually excellent—pretty and touching. David seemed to be enjoying it more than me. He laughed aloud here and there, looked over at me to see if I was enjoying it. And I was. Enough. Still, I was more focused on what was in my bag and what her reaction would be. Would she think it was funny? Would she think *I* was funny?

I looked around at the audience. At 60, I was delighted to be on the younger curve of the crowd. It was like dining at Della Femina's or visiting my Uncle Jimmy at the nursing home, minus the wheelchairs and the drooling. When it was over, the sisters took to the stage. Leapt right up from the audience, both perky, droll brunettes, they sat on stools as a moderator with a microphone called for questions or comments. I had nothing to say, nothing to ask, and I realized all of a sudden, crestfallen, that my books would go unsigned. The surprise in my bag a silly embarrassment. It was not the forum I expected. There was not the interaction I was hoping for. I thought, crestfallen, as I watched her in her signature cowl-neck top, exposing her hateful neck and also her shoulders and clavicles, I thought, she's a little self-effacing. A little, who me? Which is surprising because she's so accomplished and comes from such amazing stock, humor heritage of the highest order: the daughter of Phoebe and Henry Ephron, the writing team responsible for the Nick and Nora movies. Oh, I get it. They named Nora after Nora. But what of Delia? Who's she named after? It must be hard to be Delia Ephron, but I have my own sibling mishigahss.

"It's like *The Vagina Monologues* without the vaginas," Nora said from the stage and her sister nodded in agreement. What it was, was women on stage, unadorned by production values, except for an easel of crude drawings of dresses, stage left, that Linda Lavin flipped over pages to reiterate a point, about fashion, fathers, womanhood and boobs. Although I do like fashion, and I had a couple of fathers (see *My Two Dads* also further in the collection), I mostly couldn't relate. And worse, then, I realized my clever surprise in the bag would never see the light of night. What made me think I'd have an audience with her besides the audience of everyone? It's what you think, well, it's what *I* thought, because I like her and wanted to present her with my gift.

And what was that gift? OK, time to divulge, and I'm hoping here that it won't be anti-climactic. This is also what I planned to say as I presented it to her: "Since you feel bad about your neck, Nora, here's a jar of Olay Regenerist Microsculpting Cream." (I do the advertising for the brand and get it for free.) "While not surgical results, of course… (legally, we have to say this in the advertising) it does tighten the neck and firms the jaw line."

She never got to get it.

It will remain in the trunk of my car with her name on it if I ever should ever have an audience with her again.

— 2008

The Deal With Dogs

The deal with dogs is unspoken but as authentic as Alpo. The deal is: your time together is brief. Ten years, seven and a half years, thirteen years—I know people whose dogs became road kill when they were just puppies. What is a life-span? As my father once said, "you don't measure a life in chronological years, but in love years."

Puccini is 7½ years old as he lays hooked up to tubes in an intensive care unit at the Animal Medical Center on East 62nd Street. That makes him, by that trusted analogy, 52. He is beautiful. OK, all dog owners think their dogs are beautiful. Trust me. Puccini is beautiful. Human-like, with lips and green eyes and, I repeat, all dog owners think their dogs are beautiful and all dogs are beautiful. Puccini just happens to be more so.

He's Italian. Found on-line from a breeder in Italy by David, my partner. The breed—lagotto romagnolo, bred for hunting truffles. He even looked a little like a pig with a snout and a snort and those pink lips!

(The deal is: they die. Younger and sooner than you want them to.)

Puccini was picked up by David in Milan. He was small enough to fit under the seat on the flight back to New York, and occupied himself by chewing on a headset, the attendants fawning all over him. He came into our lives, this dot of a dog, all nervous energy, scampering around, sniffing, curious, then dead asleep, heaving, sighing, snoring, wincing. Out East, at our beach house in Amagansett, the water dog in him emerged. He would bound for the shore and lap it up—slogging from ocean to pool to dune to our bed, soggy, sandy, messy. Magnificent. Italian, his preferred shoes to chew were Prada. He got pasta Bolognese. He drank rosé. We treated him like an extremely hairy person. He got lobster and eggs and paté and pieces of pastries. He was a very happy dog. Also, as years wore on, a chubby one, too.

He has never bared his teeth, as dogs do, if you get in the way of them and a bone. He is shy in front of other dogs except if they are small, then he cowers and crouches, adorable, as he sniffs their muzzles and backsides. He grew from that dot to almost 50 pounds, his vet saying it isn't exactly cute when these dogs get older and they get diabetes, but he got smoked duck breast and Cap'n Crunch. (Note: this is not exactly a cautionary tale. Not to say do not spoil these creatures who look to us with such trust and such faith.)

I always think of this: We moved once when we had two other dogs. We packed vans and boxes and realized how much stuff we had. The dogs had nothing but a collar and a leash each. Two bowls and a box of Milkbones. Profoundly struck by this, I said to a friend: "we have so much, they have so little," and she said, "oh, no, they have your love" and it doesn't exactly sound so profound now. But it is, and it was, and it will always be.

Puccini, year one, year two. What a handful, what a spunky, scrappy, gorgeous dog, who demands you stroke him, feed him, love him or just be with him. We'd leave him, for hours as we went to work. We never knew what he did to occupy himself besides sleeping—we have a small terrace and he was trained early on to relieve himself out there, genius that he is. Rarely did he eat his odorless, boring, brittle Eukanuba pellets—he waited for the Perdue chicken nuggets in the fun, dinosaur shapes. And the pizza. And he got them because he waited and he whined and wouldn't take no for an answer. Peanut butter tucked into shank bones, that was a trick a trainer said would keep him occupied while I was reading the paper.

Back in the Star Again

He was always there at my feet, and when quickly done with the peanut butter, he would drop that bone like a brick on my feet. He was hungry. He loved food. He got everything.

"Be careful. He's got to lose some weight. He's cute now, but in a few years..."

Popcorn and bananas and bagels with lox and cream cheese. Tomatoes.

Not a cautionary tale?

We traveled while he sat in kennels, waiting patiently on concrete floors. As opposed to the 6,000 thread count sheets and down duvet covers he normally slept on. (He lets us sleep in the bed with him.) He is pissed when we return tanned and revitalized, while he was deprived of cheese. Eventually, he forgives us for leaving him. And he gets fed. And loved. And fed. And fed.

Puccini, round, robust, started to resemble a pig more and more with his snout and his snorts. We were suckers for him, slaves to his every culinary whim. (In the elevator in our building, we meet up with a doctor and his dog, Austin. A moody poodle, his owner says, who is on Prozac. Austin, dark with his black coat, gazes straight ahead in the elevator, depressed, while Puccini pants and poses and wags his tail, thunk, thunk, against the elevator wall, mouth open, eyes wide, anticipating everything. "Don't mind Austin," the doctor would say. "If only he had one

The Deal With Dogs

shred of Puccini's happiness.")

Everyone wanted to know what breed he was, some cocka-mamie-poodle? He is his own. Brown and white, panda-faced, wolf-man like. Puccini. How does one say *joie de vivre* in Italian? *Joie de vivio*? But then, one day, he threw up buckets and wouldn't eat, tail drooping, eyes cloudy, excreting. He went from exuberant to half-dead in an absolute minute. Not eating. Not interested. Drinking gallons from the pool and the toilet. Rabid-looking. Dazed. Hiding in the far reaches of beach house, in places he'd never retreated to. On the 4th of July, we thought he had gotten out. Whistles and cries of "Here boy!" went unanswered. No Puccini until ninety minutes later when I heard the small tinkle of his dog tags and we found him wedged between a 50-foot cedar and the deer fencing at an outer edge of the property. That same father of mine once told me: "Dogs go off, far from their masters, to die."

But, wait, there's more! A miracle. He came back from the near-dead. We got him to the intensive care unit of the Animal Medical Center. And five days later, miracle of miracles, he was back home with us. Recovered. Requiring insulin injections daily and on a strict Science Diet. No snacks. No treats. No foie gras.

He is beautiful and alive and ours once again. A new lease on life, but for how long? One more happy night is a beautiful bargain now but we hope to have many more happy nights with Puccini on our pillows. Nights and, hopefully years. The suddenness of his illness was frightening. His five-day recovery, astounding. So this is the point: DON'T FEED YOUR DOG YOUR FOOD.

A cautionary tale after all.

— 2009

My Two Dads

I am not a Guatemalan boy or an Asian girl adopted by a couple of gay guys. I am a 61-year old man. My two fathers were this way: one was biological, who died when I was a year old in 1949; the other was my stepfather, a man who sported a pistol on his belt, a fat cigar like FDR, a hat with a feather tucked into the band, and who turned out to be the most generous, loving person I will ever know.

Two fathers. One story.

It is Father's Day. No time like the present to be sentimental about fathers. In my case, fathers who are gone and long gone. Let's start with the stepfather who took us all on—Mom, four of us kids, me, the youngest—back when they married in 1955. We called him Eddie, not Pop, or Dad, or even Father or anything affectionate.

He always wanted to hug us and we were continually straining away from his grasps. We were resentful and hurting and wanting our real father although none of us four ever said any of this to any of us or to our mother as far as I knew. "You're not my father," we would taunt, me the bratty boy, with my tongue out, my thumbs in my ears, fingers splayed. And he took it. Eddie took it.

"*You're not my father.*"

Yet I was his boy, while the older ones of us were getting married and moving out of the house not long after he arrived. My older sister and brother, long into their teens when Eddie came along, were deep into their own lives and in a few years had their own families. My second sister was 11 when Eddie first came and he tried real hard to win her over and I can't be sure he succeeded there. I was seven when he was thrown into our fully formed family. Formed by a tragedy left behind by the first father.

I don't mean to be partial to one, but the original one I never knew. Here's what I can piece together and recall: there's a picture of him looking high, it's black and white, Harry Truman was president, there's a glass of what looks like scotch on the rocks in front of Raymond. Raymond, the first father, my genes his. I was occasionally told that Raymond liked to drink. And to sing! I know this from one photograph, black and white with a narrow white scalloped border. He's in his shirtsleeves, looking shit-faced, but happy and blurry. He's wearing glasses—thick lenses, wire-frames, a big smile on his face. There's another photo I remember, or just fantasize or may even pretend to remember. In this one, he wears a grey fedora, although it could have been brown, or dark blue. This is another black and white photo, taken on a second-story rooftop in Brooklyn in Bensonhurst where I was born. And then this third photo. Before I was born. The gorgeous, glamorous photo is what makes me think he was happy. Or, anyway, that night. It's an engagement party at the Copacabana nightclub in the 1940s. Big. Glossy. Black and white. A folder of a photo. A large, rectangular keepsake photo one opens like a four page book. On the outside, against a background of shiny white, is a quick illustration of a haughty show girl, just her face, with stylized lines of poofy red hair. She looks indifferent, this Miss Copacabana, her shoulder lifted up against her chin. Her eyes closed. Inside, is a group shot. Six couples in the picture, three on each side of a table. Brothers and sisters and in-laws. A gardenia is in the hair of the engaged girl. Mom and Dad face into the camera, he's wearing those wire-framed glasses, his eyes hard to see. Her dress low cut and floral—it must have been summer. World War II was over and they were newlyweds celebrating a sister-in-law's engagement, Woody Allen could do a movie around this folder photograph. I have seen it, this one for sure, and see it still when I close my eyes, all details, the glasses, the cigarettes.

Raymond died in a train accident not too long afterwards. He was 37 or 38.

"Was it a suicide?" I finally got up the courage to ask my mother. I was 19 then, in therapy, and forced by my therapist to finally confront my Mom with this. She had a cigarette going, she always had a cigarette going, stained dark red at the filter tip, a Pall Mall Gold 100. She smoked one hundred of them a day and eventually gave them up for emphysema. "What makes you think it was a suicide?" she asked, tapping the cigarette in the black plastic ashtray, looking this way and that, a cup of coffee steaming in front of her. "I don't know why I think it. Except it seems so unexplained, the death." "Why go there?" She crashed the cigarette in the ashtray. It was never much discussed again. Not with her. Hardly with anyone who knew him. Taboo. He was dead and long gone, Eddie was present and wanting us, all of us, to love him.

Anyway, Eddie was a softie. A softie sporting a pistol. A paradox, but to me, I never really saw his aggressive, gun side. He's dead ten years now. And as he lay sick and dying, I was finally able to express to him how I finally felt, at the end of it all, the second father dead. What he had done. To thank him for being the father that chose us rather than bore us. A softie, and here's two examples:

1—When he got really mad at me his preferred tactic of

threat was behind small clenched teeth—" I'll mop the floor with you!"—laughable, really, I was to be turned on my head, my hair as mop, draped across the floor. Like a Fred and Ginger dance more than a threat.

2—I once screamed at my sister Judy and called her a bitch. She ran to Eddie and ratted on me, how I cursed at her. He came to me, unhitching his belt (he unhitched it a lot and never used it) and said to me: "What did you say, what was that curse?" And I admitted the word was: hell. I told him I told her to go to hell. "That's not so terrible," he said, low, under his breath, a whisper to me. He put his belt back on and me, staying upstairs, trying to overhear the outcome of Judy and Eddie downstairs, nervous and frightened. "That's not so terrible, Judy. Hell." "He told you hell?" Judy said. "No, no. It was the b word!" He came back up. He was laughing, trying to hug me. I think he thought the whole thing was kind of cute. "You and me, pal," he seemed to say with the laughter. "We'll protect each other from the women." I was all of nine then. I didn't hug him back (you're not my father!) but, looking back, I think that was our turning point. Our threshold to pals. I wonder, all these years later, if it wasn't his plan of getting closer. Like brothers rather than stepfather and stepson.

The unknowable Raymond, on the other hand, is a completely different scenario. No hugs to retreat from, no shared intimacies, no collusion against the girls. Not much of nothing. But I have a second-hand idea or two of him. Once, by chance, coming across a box of memories, I reasoned he was a softie, too. A romantic. He was a traveling salesman, his region, I put together from fragments of snippets of overheard conversations, from DC to Boston, the Northeast Corridor now. On that train, in between Pennsylvania Stations, he died. On the train one minute, on the tracks the next.

One boring Saturday, my Mom helping out with paperwork in Eddie's shoe store, the house quiet and all my own, I was rummaging through my Mom's closet and came across a shoe box filled with cards. As I opened it, a scent rose up at me, like rust, like pages in an old book. I opened one card with a padded, three-dimensional red felt heart on the front, some printed lines of Valentine affection, and then a signature, blue ink on the bottom, I touched it, skimmed the handwriting, hoping to feel something. It read: *All my love, Ray.* Who was this man? What did they share, husband and wife, Mom and Dad, Esther and Raymond? Another old photograph I once saw: my Mom, lying on her bed, a towel covering her somewhat, and she looks so playful, her legs bent, her knees slightly separated. She's laughing, suggestively. Had to be Raymond who took this picture. Black and white. Did they have sex a lot? It was inconceivable and, once again, unknowable. I couldn't possibly imagine it or dwell on it too long, it embarrasses me in fact. That photograph taken also before I was born. All I have of Dad #1 are pictures, very few, including the one he must have taken of my Mom on the bed. But I think of him almost every time I have a glass of wine. A good, if empty, moment to remember.

The dirty, rotten shame of the first father, the fact that he is unknowable to me, is now, I am sure, something I helped create out of my own fears. My earliest memories of me, fatherless, even after Eddie came into the picture, is how I believed no one ever wanted to talk about the tragedy. Too painful an event for anyone to want to relive or ever refer to. I know I was given signals to not discuss it. So I didn't. But I wondered, always wondered what happened on that mysterious train during that mysterious August night in 1949. And then, there's this to consider—the stepfather turns out to be a set-up date with Mom by the dead father's baby brother! Uncle Abie, who is still alive and offers still no insight about his brother's death. Suicide? Foul play? An accident? "All we know is that the insurance company paid and so suicide has been ruled out," Abie has said. As far as the insurance company is concerned, but I keep thinking...

And now, 60 years on, it all starts to fade. Fade a little. The how, the why of that death.

I am not a father. My brother Ike, perhaps in compensation for his early fatherlessness, turns out to be the best father on the planet. With the exception of Eddie, who I did wind up calling Pop and Dad alternatively, and eventually, as he succumbed to pancreatic cancer.

These fathers. Men who have formed who I am with absence and with extraordinary presence. I finally called #2 Dad—*Dad*! in utter awe and appreciation of how he waited and waited until I came around and understood all he had done. And all he was. From bringing in puppies, to taking me and only me out for Sunday rides in his small motorboat moored in Sheepshead Bay, to helping with the down payment on my weekend house. For loving my moody mother and telling me I could do anything I chose to do. When he was dying, his death not instantaneous, but drawn out for two and a half years, I got the chance to thank him, tearfully, and with hugs I initiated, and all the time. You *are* my father, with your different last name and our polar opposite appearances.

These are two men I miss. One I will always wonder about. The other who was a wonder to me.

— 2009

If You Want To Feel 100

If you want to feel 100 years old, go to the Surf Lodge in Montauk. Montauk has not seen the likes of this happening hipness since the Rolling Stones checked into the Memory Motel. Or since Andy Warhol was in residence. Love it or hate it (and many love to hate it), it is what it is. Motel. Outdoor bar overlooking the gleaming, tranquil Fort Pond. Restaurant so bathed in turquoise blue it could be underwater. But what it mostly is is IT. I understand vans come in from Southampton, peopled with young women in Pucci sundresses and Havaianas flip-flops, 20-somethings paying something like $200 for the trip to hip. In search of what? In search of NOW.

Now, don't get me wrong. I am hip and happening enough. I have carefully trimmed facial hair, a pair of

Hermés sandals that set me back a cool $600, and a beach house in Amagansett with a sexy pool. I do the elliptical machine at Body Tech often. I am also, often, desperately, a la mode. So to speak.

Let's be honest. It's a struggle at my age.

The world—Surf Lodge this moment, Gossip Girl, Speidi, Zac Efron, Miley Cyrus and/or Hannah Montana, caters to the young. As youth is wasted on, incidentally, in that old sawhorse of a cliché.

Bear with me. I was once 30. I went to Studio 54 and had a good, good time, I think. Oh the blissful blur of the 70s. I look back on that Hy from on high at 61 and remember, and cling to him. *I had my time.* Clearly, at Surf Lodge, in the year of, oh lord, 2009, it is no longer my time. *Mr. Cellophane*, a clever, if sad number from Kander & Ebb's *Chicago*, about a man who gets no notice is how I felt the other evening at Surf Lodge. How I often feel in this universe.

Bebel Gilberto was scheduled to appear and it was a late June evening of warmth and sun. OK—so maybe not all the women were in their '20s in those flirty sundresses and ubiquitous flip-flops. And maybe all the guys, in porkpie hats, tight knee-length plaid shorts and flip-flops, too, were not all in their early '30s. But it sure looked that way to me.

It was the rare spotting of a guy with a head full of gray hair and when I spotted him, there was a brief exchange of furtive glance that spoke volumes in a nanosecond: "What are you doing here? Don't you realize we are not catered to here? Don't you see how everyone else, is staring down a décolletage or surveying an ass? What business do we have here?"

Gratefully, a pseudo-celebrity showed up, stylish in her flirty sundress, the flip-flops, but surprisingly, in need of a root touch-up. She's 50ish and a Mom now. She's busy and beauty maintenance is very time-consuming, even for guys! But she raised the age quotient up. But just a drop because she was outnumbered by a hundred other girls, younger girls by decades with a similar style and those freaking flip-flops! with no need to conceal grey hairs. They would breeze past me, a mojito, a dark and stormy in hand…in search of what? In search of who? Somebody famous, somebody rich, somebody sexy. Somebody young. (Somebody not me.)

Happily, you can't feel like a centenarian at Della Femina's. In fact, there, I feel a little like chicken. Jerry Della Femina is a hoot (he's 73 if he's a day) and his restaurant is lovely. A suggestion, Jerry, considering your demographic, also mindful of this economy: Early Bird Dinner Special, half off, 4:30 p.m. works for me. And you can forget the dinner and a movie idea that Nick & Toni's offers in the off season. It's hard for me to stay awake for a movie in the evening.

Speaking of Nick & Toni's, you can feel fine there. It's a

Back in the Star Again

very mixed bag. Old, young, gay straight. Even the wait staff and the help run the gamut. But Tom, the bartender, is young enough to be my grandson. Handsome and tall. Trim and glib. Australian, to add to his accented appeal. He's everything you wish you were except he's stuck there, at the wrong side of the bar, working.

The Laundry Restaurant, where Amagansett and East Hampton converge, is a favorite. People come in behind walkers, with canes. Or maybe it's just that I tend to have dinner there at around the time the kids are having a late lunch. Listen. When you get up at 5 a.m. you get hungry for dinner at 5 p.m. Those clocks are stubbornly reset as you get older. Sleeping in for me is now 7 a.m. The latest.

Rowdy Hall isn't about walkers but strollers. Booster chairs abound; it's often chock full of children. I sit at the bar there, alone, and write. I close my eyes and pretend it's still O'Malley's, where I would sit at the bar with a burger and a burgundy, dumbstruck that 30 years have passed in a minute.

Then there's the Blue Parrot. I've never been, but I just read in Page Six that Jon Bon Jovi, an investor, was there over the 4th of July. I've seen him at the East Hampton Palm, he's not young anymore, either. Famous, yes. But also 50ish. And Renée Zellweger, who I understand is also a partner, is now 40. Ron Perlman, another owner, is eligible for Social Security should he need it. And should it be there.

And the point is?

If You Want To Feel 100

I'm not sure—but let's try this on for size.

I am a baby boomer. The early bunch of them, born in 1948. We are Bill, Hillary. We are Liza and Cher and Bette. We are Hamptonites like Alec Baldwin, Matt Lauer, Katie Couric and Jay McInerney. We are Al Gore and Lesley Gore. We are the world. Yet, I feel like we are the invisible generation now. Mr. and Mrs. and Ms. Cellophane. Too downturned to retire. Once flush, now forlorn. Forgotten.

Not interested in being Donny Downer, or even Donny Deutsch, let's move on.

American Hotel, Sag Harbor. It's dark in that front bar room. Darkness at noon. I like that. I've been contemplating botox for my forehead which features both vertical and horizontal creases. Even in repose, my forehead is a field of furrows. In the dim light of the gorgeous American Hotel front dining room, (stay away from the sky lit room to your right) in the fall with a fire going, the art deco posters on the wall, you've stepped into the 1920s and you were not born then. Darkness, plus deco, makes me look and feel younger.

I go there a lot.

But it's hard to avoid the Surf Lodge. Montauk is not as far from where I live in Amagansett as Southampton is. I'm certainly not going to The Pink Elephant. And the other clubs…I know there's something on Three Mile Harbor Road…and the Star Room ne Swamp looks like it's reopening? I remember the Hampton Attic, a straight friend of mine jokingly referred to it as the Hampton Closet (not funny). And the Stephen Talkhouse, right there in Amagansett, is something I pass by at 9 p.m., my partner David driving, me dozing, and think and sometimes smirk: *I had my time.*

My time. Us boomers, now, more likely, busters, can look back, at least, at when we were young and thin and able to stay up all night long with or without a stimulus package of powder.

The Surf Lodge? I may get noticed if I decide to don a Pucci sundress, a pair of flip-flops, size 12. A ridiculous cowboy hat.

I am trying for a new look now, for some absurd reason—no, the reason is to be noticed. '70s porn star is the look I'm after, a moustache drooping down to my jawline. Think *Starsky & Hutch*. *CHiPS*. Tom Selleck in *Magnum P.I.* Except the 'stache is much more salt than pepper. Gabby Hayes comes to mind in a mirror.

It doesn't help that my paunch grows more pronounced year by year, and my hair is receding and startlingly silver.

There is no way to relive what I deep-down know I cannot.

I'm down with that. Or down *by* that.

Or something like that.

— 2009

Puccini, Part 2

If you follow this column, you may remember Puccini, Star dog who first appeared here in the April 30th issue of Guestwords. He was alive in that story.

It was written last July, shortly after his harrowing and heartbreaking recovery from pancreatitis. Diabetes was also diagnosed then. We were shooting him up with insulin twice a day. Restricting him, for the most part, to gooey, pungent Science Diet meals.

He's very much alive today, just not in the physical sense. He's alive in our hearts, mine and David's, his owners, his devoted slaves. He's alive in that specific corner, that exact spot in our apartment, there, against the wall, there, beside the bed. He's alive in the cool hole he digs in the sandy Amagansett dune that is, that was, his front yard.

He's there, at the foot of the bed while we slept. There at our heads on the pillows when it was time for his morning walk.

He's also there during a thunderstorm, when he would scramble into the bathtub, quivering. There when the noon siren rang, which he would howl along with.

Mostly, he's alive in what he has influenced: his unabashed generosity of love, his unwavering positiveness, everything about him that reduces me to a puddle of tears.

He died on my birthday—something symmetrical there, something spiritual. I look for further meaning—who wouldn't? because he came and went, such a powerful presence, in a scant eight and a half years.

At last count, there are approximately 250 million dogs (homeless and living on Further Lane) in America. A little less than one dog per person.

Puccini was one in 250 million to us.

When he got sick and almost died over the July 4th weekend of last year, I thought: was this our doing? We fed him table scraps and more—David cooked for him, he got leftovers, he got everything—were we killing him with kindness?

No. We were indulging him the way you would a child. What can you give a dog? Not a Harvard education, not a cell phone, not a cool pair of shoes. Yet they are as much our children as our children. But way less demanding and they never, ever blame you for anything.

Pucini, Part 2

Puccini.

So named because he was Italian, lagotto romagnolo the breed, an Italian water dog, the brown and white 'cousin' to the Obamas 'Bo', Puccini bred for hunting truffles—we would take him to Dean & DeLuca to get a whiff of what his job was supposed to be.

Once there, once anywhere, heads would turn. Kids, grown up men and women, would kneel down to his level and look straight into his hypnotic, green eyes. Stroke him. Want to know him. He loved the attention—who wouldn't? He was spoiled and pampered. Not a pet, a prize.

Puccini. Who seemed always to have this imaginary exclamation point floating above his curly head until just before he died.

Until just before he died, he had the strength and the interest to grab hold of a biscuit and bound up to our tall bed in New York and chomp on it. Grateful. Spilling crumbs and drool. Content with the smallest of things. A purple plastic bone that floated in the pool he'd retrieve over and over again. Dive in. Bring it back out. Triumphant. How happy, how willing dogs are to please. (A squeaky toy he'd demolish in minutes, triumphantly, once again, dropping the squeaky mechanism at our feet for approval. Panting. Proud.)

Puccini.

The companion who never complained. The bud who

never got bored.

So he got food. So he begged, annoyingly, at dinner time. So he needed to be put outside in Amagansett while we entertained, served our guests lobster and chicken and pasta, me keeping a watchful eye on him, his wet, pink nose pressed up against the glass door, mouth open, breathless, as if in the throes of an orgasm.

When the guests left, he got a shred of lobster, a bit of chicken. A smoked almond or two. So what? He went to bed as contented as us. Satisfied. Grateful.

In the morning, he got his beach exercise, sniffing the remnants of crabs and cookouts and what all else. Once back home, he dug a small hole in the same dune, breathed deeply his same satisfied sigh, and slept. Secure. Content.

And now he's gone. After a joyful, exuberant further nine months since his diabetes diagnosis, he's now gone. He went quickly downhill during a weekend in April when we opened back our Amagansett house where he, somewhat impaired, losing his eyesight (eight and a half years, 60ish in the human equation) still tucked himself into his shallow bit of dune. And still, the few days before he left us, he led us to the ocean, lolled in it, led us there as he always did, tail wagging, tongue panting.

He didn't require us to put him down, we didn't need to make that painful decision. He never asked much of us except us. He left quietly, mercifully. He just stopped

Pucini, Part 2

breathing. Quietly. Painlessly.

The quiet comfort of dogs. What are they thinking? What are they feeling?

He just went.

You lose a dog and you lose a connection to a more awe-inspiring reality. People are never so forgiving. Other animals not nearly as connecting.

Dogs, Puccini in particular, came into our lives and profoundly, silently, gorgeously, taught us how to be humble, how to be generous, how to be patient. How to expect nothing but a bone, a beggin' strip, a leftover filet mignon from the Palm.

Puccini is buried in a towel that we used to dry him off from his water romps. Right there, by the pool he swam laps in. He is memorialized under an engraved stone. And now, here.

He trusted us and he gave us the world. Required nothing but our complete attention, those walks on the beach. And yes, the Palm.

There are other dogs.

There will be other dogs.

But there is only one Puccini.

— 2010

What I Do

These days, this year—my 42nd in advertising, I am working at Saatchi & Saatchi on the consumer products giant, Procter & Gamble. Specifically on the Olay account (formerly Oil of Olay). Procter people based in Cincinnati, Ohio, have their own catch-phrases and they have been called a cult, dogged by that spooky 13-star logo. They are known as Proctoids, and here is what a lot of them say in meetings: "At the end of the day…" "Having said that…" "…engage…"—they use engage when referring to the consumer. Gone is "let's run it up the flagpole and see who salutes it"—that phrase may be featured on *Mad Men* as they move their story line through the 1960s. Proctoids also end most of their sentences with their last few words rising up in the air like birds taking flight, like

What I Do

a question is being asked even though one isn't. Maybe it's a Midwest thing. Maybe it's just me.

Me.

I am a copywriter. I was called an 'ace writer' once in an ad gossip rag when I left one job for another. (I saved that circled-in-red blurb in a bunch of hard copies.) I have been called 'boy wonder' and a legend, too—that last reference made mostly by myself. I have also been called down to HR for being too aggressive. And, also been called out of it, as I got fired over and over in the '70s, the '80s, the '90s. But I'm still here, as Stephen Sondheim says. A writer. A lover of the business of advertising that has given me a voice, a career, a confidence, a beach house, and the world.

Morocco and Sydney. A seaside resort outside of Rome. Prague. Malaga, Madrid and Miami. Endless LA. Lots of Chicago. The world on shoots. When you're a copywriter you not only write the commercials, you also travel the world supervising their filming. Boon-doggley some would say and sometimes, that's so. Especially when it comes fairly easily to me. The shoots, the travel—you get to be a part of all the details, the wardrobe, the casting, the locations, you and your art director. The team. The team that Bill Bernbach back in that *Mad Men* moment, decreed that a writer and an art director should work together, collaborate, like George and Ira Gershwin, like Rudolf Nureyev and Margot Fonteyn. The team. Like a marriage of sorts.

Back in the Star Again

How did it all happen? How did I stumble into this long, lucrative career? A career that finds me saying no to Stockard Channing as a voice-over candidate for Olay. (you can call it Oil of Olay, and you will, but check the packaging—'Oil of' is gone a decade) Saying no to Bernadette Peters and Patti LuPone. No to Victor Garber and Mandy Patinkin. And yes to Christine Lahti.

How?

Return with us, well, with me, to the prehistoric late '60s. Hymo, that's the nickname given to me as a late teenager attending the School of Visual Arts, me, a painter, a drawer, an Orthodox Sephardic Jew born in Brooklyn, finding myself in a college on 23rd Street in Manhattan during the era of acid and big Bohemia. Me, barely out of wearing a yarmulke and a talis, me, confused and raw, somehow found my way to THE SCHOOL OF VISUAL ARTS! How'd that happen? It just did. Looking back, as this piece is wont to do, it feels like destiny. Life, whether you are there for it, or retreating from it, whether you're choosing goals or just following where fate leads, it seems like it was all predetermined somehow. Now I don't want to get all spiritual and religious, but from a yeshiva background and then a brief stint at the ultra-conservative Brooklyn College, I wound up at the School of Visual Arts in a drawing class on a bright Wednesday afternoon, drawing people, as comfortable as they can be, and as naked as the day they were born, while sitting next to a chain-smoking LSD freak in a beret.

SVA was run this way in those years: Year one was called Foundation, the groundwork laid for a variety of artistic futures and careers—the courses included 2-D design, photography, and illustration. During year two, you specialize. As I took the subway from Brooklyn to Manhattan that year (1966; I was 18) I was transfixed by the ads on the platforms and in the cars. *You Don't Have to Be Jewish to Love Levy's* with pictures of African Americans and American Indians eating a rye bread sandwich. *You can't eat atmosphere*—this for Horn & Hardart, the old automat fast food chain. And take note: the 'atmosphere' depicted in the visual is a swath of carpet to resemble a Salisbury steak, orange candles to look like carrots and a green drapery tassel mimicking broccoli. And also, Benson & Hedges 100s. *Oh, the disadvantages of our new, longer cigarette* picturing a silver cigarette case, the cigarettes crushed and extended out of the case, encircled with a rubber band to hold it together. Now I don't know about you, but those ads and the television commercials of the day—Alka Seltzer, Volkswagen— knocked me out. Called out to me. I wanted to be a part of that. It was unclear what I wanted to do exactly, how I wanted to be involved, connected to that work, but since I drew and I painted, I figured I would be an art director.

Back in the Star Again

So. Year Two SVA. I majored in advertising. And my days were filled with art director classes, print design, storyboard frame illustration, and still, a life drawing class perfecting our nudes. And then, two hours a week on a Thursday morning, a course called Copywriting. At an art school, the writing class was rather second-class. But the instructor, a practicing copywriter working at Young & Rubicam—let's call him John because his name was John—took an interest in me and my writing and one day, in the spring of 1968, the week that Martin Luther King got shot, John said to me: "You should be a writer." Five words that opened up the universe to me.

I didn't really get the distinction; I was dense in those days. I just had this vague desire to do the ads and since I was an artist, I thought I'd be involved in the art end and didn't much think of the distinction. "Who's more important in the process? The writer or the art director?" I wanted to know. "Look at it this way," John answered. "You go to a movie and you see the credits. How big is the art director credit? How prominent is the writer credit?" The art director gets a line in a field of credits, the writer has a credit all to himself.

Hmmm, I thought. Little did I realize even then that the art director works way harder, spends lots more time in an office than the copywriter does.

Sold.

Next big bit of advice from the Y&R guy, a mentor for sure though I wouldn't have realized it then or even knew of such a thing: "Get yourself to a journalism college. You might feel frustrated here with all the art majors. Or, get yourself a job!"

When he asked me where I wanted to work, I said without missing a beat: Doyle Dane Bernbach. The agency that changed advertising for the better sometime in the aforementioned *Mad Men* '60s. Bill Bernbach, the short, grey-haired, accountant-looking creative head of the agency, was credited as the first person to design the collaboration of art director and writer. Before him, a writer would slip a sheet of yellow copy paper under the art director's door and there was an ad, a TV storyboard. Bernbach put them in a room together and the division of duties got blurred. As an art person who was pointed towards copy, I found the blurring a desirable option. I was putting a 'book' (that's a portfolio of work, pre-website, way pre-tech) together. My book was a series of acetate sleeves, spiral bound, inside a leather or plastic case with handles. Inside those sleeves were ads drawn (by me). Visuals depicted with colored pencils or those pungent magic markers and a block of type, the headline and body copy typewritten on a facing acetate sleeve.

I was doing fake ads in the classes at SVA. And the Y&R guy was helping me once a week on the side, critiquing body copy (that's the text usually at the bottom of an ad) and giving me further assignments like a private tutor would. Except I didn't have to pay him. And I could never repay him.

By some miracle, I did get a job at Doyle Dane—it came to be known as that, shorthand. I took my book to a guy named Leon Meadow, a silver-haired gentleman with a missing finger joint, and he hired me! I was 20. I wore a grey Edwardian suit to the interview. I placed a small glass globe in my pocket for luck. I got the job with a handful of ads in those acetate sleeves. My favorite follows. Y&R guy said write an ad about a book you liked. I remember really liking *Rosemary's Baby* by Ira Levin, before the Mia Farrow/Roman Polanski movie came out. The book spooked me and moved me. I read it a few times and then I wrote the line: *If you're pregnant, you won't have the stomach for it.* Meaning the book. And the visual was my meticulous drawing of that paperback. I got hired right there at that interview and as soon as I left I called Y&R guy from a phone booth and told him, breathless: "I got a job at Doyle Dane Bernbach!" He was silent, then proud and pleased, I think, but also depressed. He said: "Congratulations, Hy. I've been trying to get into that agency for years!"

I was on my way, but I didn't quite know it just then. I had a job. For $6,500 a year. And I was told because I was so young and so green, that if in six months time I couldn't do the caliber of work in the real world as I had shown in those acetate sleeves, I would be let go. I was OK with that. When you're young, and basically unformed as I was with this outsized desire, you can agree to anything as long as it takes you somewhere new and shows you something better.

June 3, 1968. Day one of my big, sprawling, wonderful, diverse and roller-coaster advertising career. My office extension was 8585 and due to my alphabetical go-to-the-head-of-the-class last name, I was the first name in the black faux leather bound Doyle Dane telephone directory.

I had a small office without a window. No cube, this was long before cubicles were created. A real office, with a Royal typewriter, battleship grey and bigger than a bread box. I was put on the Polaroid account and, as with starting writers, given trade ads to do—ads not for the general public, but ads that ran in business publications for insurance companies and casting agents and people other than you and me. I remember one of the very first ads I wrote that got produced was geared to those insurance agents to convince them to take a Polaroid of a house that underwent flood damage, or a car a tree fell on. I wrote the ad: *Write about it and you may be wrong about it.* I was big on word plays, you may already be getting that idea. I can't remember what all else I wrote during those first six months but I do remember telling Mr. Missing-Digit-Joint-Meadow for some reason, "I'm

Back in the Star Again

too young to be working on this." And I got switched to the Volkswagen account. Just like that. Sometimes, so many things came to me so easily and just by asking. Squeaky wheel syndrome? Fate? Luck? Timing?

I never thought of myself as ambitious and I still don't. Desirous, not ambitious. But I made that move onto VW and never looked back. All of a sudden I was catapulted into the fame that the ad biz allows. In two years time, I racked up a series of awards for my work on Volkswagen that impressed even me. The ads I wrote aren't important. They were continuing images and headlines in a style that a guy named Helmut Krone art directed and Julian Koenig wrote—*Lemon, Think small,* etc. Iconic work that holds up even today as being self-effacing and clever. Word plays and subtleties. A favorite of mine done by the senior team the VW baton got passed to—Roy Grace and John Noble, art director and writer—*There are a lot of cars for $3,400. This is two of them.* Black and white overhead shot of a black and a white beetle. *There's no place like car.* For the camper. And on and on.

Volkswagen in the '60s and then the '70s, ruled the awards shows and I got my share. I was not yet 22 and there I was, in a tuxedo at the New York Hilton, accepting an award. A gold typewriter key encased in a chunky block of Lucite. Our Oscar, this Gold Key. And on top of that, that golden year, 1969, I won a silver key. Second place, less chunky. The typewriter key enclosed inside was just a disc without the typewriter key appendage. This, for a Sara Lee coupon ad entitling the bearer to 10 cents off: *Save bread on our rolls* my headline read. It was the '60s. I moonlighted from Volkswagen to Sara Lee. And a Clairol product called Great Day, a men's hair coloring. *More and more men with grey hair are combing the streets* I wrote, to some acclaim (another award) convincing men that grey hair leads to unemployment and searching for work. Combing the streets. Oh how interesting it was, how powerful it was to work at Doyle Dane Bernbach at that time. Anything went. Anything. No client said no or even boo. They wanted to buy what we were selling so that they could be selling cars and rolls and hair coloring. We were riding the crest of creativity that Doyle Dane created. All of us. I just happened to be the youngest of us at the time.

El Al Airlines was another ground-breaking account at the time. *My son, the pilot.* Sony, another. And here, the word plays really abound. *Telefishin'*—an ad for a small portable TV, with a picture of a guy in black and white, watching the tiny tube with a satisfied smirk in a canoe with a fishing rod. The last line of the ad read: *And if the fish aren't biting, you can always catch Robert Trout* (for the younger and uninformed, Robert Trout was the Katie Couric of his day. On WCBS-TV News, cable still decades away.)

These ads done at the very place I was working, inspired

me and informed my writing. I was developing a style. Borrowed, but also tweaked to be my own. Some would say pun-like and I was proud of it. The cleverness: *What to do if your Prince Charming is snow white* an ad in women's magazines for once again, Great Day men's hair coloring And one of my favorites, also done in 1969 for El Al Airlines, a trade ad to travel agents to promote Israel as a tourist destination. Visual: (black and white) a guy waterskiing with a wide wake of water behind his skis. My headline: The parting of the Red Sea, 1969. There's that yeshiva boy all grown up and facing the world of advertising squarely and head on.

Now I'm 24. Promoted to assistant copy supervisor, a fairly meaningless title but one I cherished all the same, while my salary in those four years upped to $14,500. It was the time when the cliché of Japanese photographers abounded. Often groups of Japanese men dressed in suits and bowing would tour Doyle Dane with big, bulky cameras and take pictures of all of us teams, as if they could replicate the dazzling creativity with a photograph and recreate it back home. I was also chosen to be profiled in a Japanese magazine called "Brain" and in one issue there was a photo of me and a reprint of a Sony ad of mine (*This this stereo stereo tape tape recorder recorder has has an an echo echo chamber chamber*—anything went in those days) and the article is written in Japanese so I couldn't say what it said, but it's a good picture of me and I have saved two hard copies somewhere.

Now it's 1972. I had been hearing more and more about a small boutique agency called Carl Ally, Inc. run by a guy named, duh, Carl Ally with accounts like Pan Am and Fiat. Small. Precious. I sent my book, now not acetate sleeves, but real ads and semi-famous ones at that, a dozen or so that ran in Life and Time. Many of them featured in awards annuals. I had kind of a name—names were easy to come by, all of us young 'geniuses' were always poring over awards annuals and names stuck out like kings while I was prince-like. Carl Ally's job for a young writer was paying $28,000 a year but when they saw how young I was they downsized me to $23,000. "You don't want to make all that money at your age," said the head art director, a brooding Italian type named Amil (more, much more about him later). Handsome and soft-spoken, he convinced me, I guess, that I didn't.

Now I must admit at this stage of the game, anyone who wanted me, I was theirs. It helped that in this case it was a powerful, talented agency type who I admired and felt it was my next logical move up. Time to move on from Doyle Dane Bernbach. Which at the time I thought no matter what I did there, I would always be just a kid.

I left. Told missing digit and also the creative director that I was going and they warned me. "You'll be back," the creative director said. And he was right. I was back. In a week. Culturally, Doyle Dane was family. Large and warm and comfy. Contrarily, Ally was small and cold and unwelcoming. At Doyle (even shorter-hand, as it came to be known) I graduated to a window office with my larger salary and position. At Ally, they led me to a closet-sized interior space. The noisy Xerox machine, big as a room, in the room next door, I felt lost and alone and unloved. I got a Pan Am assignment and did a silly ad and I was miserable. Oddly, in that year, Ally was experimenting with a radical four-day work week. So on my first Friday off, believing I had made a mistake, I made a call to the Doyle creative director, one Bob Levenson. He saw me that afternoon and I was reinstated. "So soon?" he said. "Yes, it was," I agreed. Back in their arms again and at the salary I left at, the Carl Ally bump not felt at all since I left in a truncated week.

Bravely, early that next Monday morning, I went into brooding Italian and said I was leaving. He was not happy. Let's face it, no one likes to be rejected. Especially not after a mere four-day week. He said: "Leave immediately." And me, sharpening my wise-guy, young-turk image, wanted here, wanted there, boldly replied—"Well, I wasn't planning on giving notice…"

Back at DDB…but not for long. Wanderlust, impatience. And a guy named Ed McCabe came calling. ED MCCABE—if you can do something larger than all caps,

What I Do

I would. Ed was it for me in those years. At 5'5", a giant. Irish and a genius at what he did and what he wrote. Often drunk, but who cared and who knew? He was Ed McCabe and nine months after I came back to Doyle I told them I was leaving again and Digit admitted that this was a much better job than that other one I had left for. I was so grateful for that honesty. I would leave and never return again to Doyle Dane Bernbach, except in my memory.

Scali, McCabe, Sloves was the agency that put Perdue Chicken on the map. The agency that gave America Volvo. Barney's was the account I was hired for. Barney's, before it was Barney's New York. It was starting to be a department store to be reckoned with in downtown New York. Like Bloomingdale's at the time but Barney's was located on 7th Avenue and 17th Street, long before Chelsea became Chelsea. Barney's then was Boystown (bar-mitzvah suits). But they were on the edge of change from bargain basement to Giorgio Armani. Fred Pressman saw the wave of European designers like Armani and Cardin, and rode that wave to become an enormous fashion player. Ed was given the task of changing the image into something special and I got hired to write the ads under him. Ed McCabe, with his irreverent New York fuck-you voice. *You can't eat atmosphere,* referred to earlier, was his line. Along with a million other in-your-face lines in the '60s. A punk-ey, drunk-ey writer. My idol after the Bernbach experience..

Back in the Star Again

The best of the best, Ed. And there I was, all of 24, reporting to him on Barney's.

It was a rough few years at Scali, McCabe. I was terrified, by Ed, his temper and his harsh criticisms of my work. He was far from easy. I was afraid of him and he knew it and he preyed on it. At least, that's how I remember it. Years later seeing Ed at a retrospective, then having a bunch of drinks with him after, I got a different perspective. He was older, mellower. I was older too, of course, and no longer frightened since I no longer worked for him. "You were one of my favorite writers, Hy. The one with the most promise," he said and I melted and wanted to hug him. And I think we did hug. Ed McCabe, who wound up firing me, the most brilliant ad writer I have ever known. Things are so large when you're young. I'm not young now, but that experience with him is still enormous. The ads I did there, oddly, were not the best. There was one line I recall for Barney's that I liked and Ed, stepping out of character (perhaps he was drunk) marched down the hall in those offices at 345 Park Avenue, hawking the line to the other creatives. When he liked something, which was rare, he pitted all of us writers against each other—his way to make us do better. As I see it now, decades later, I see it as how he was such an advocate of good ad writing no matter where it came from, although it mostly came from him.

The line? *What drives men to a clothing store they can't*

walk to? Dated, for sure by now, but then a line that led you in to all the reasons why Barney's was a 'destination.' A place to go to by subway or cab since no one lived in that neighborhood in 1973.

I also had a small, inconsequential hand in the Perdue account. I was off to the side of other forgettable accounts. After two and a half years, and a crazy moment of flexing my creativity and being the opposite of political, I got fired. The details are not important and the job didn't lead to much more recognition in the world of awards (I was so involved in wanting to win in my 20s and beyond) but there was one ad, one line that Ed wrote for Barney's that I was relegated to write the body copy for, and somewhat gratefully. *The conservative clothes are in the right wing.* Ads like this would never fly up the flagpole or otherwise today. Planners—another level of insertion between creatives and clients would find these kinds of lines not saying enough. Not strategic. But, in those years, it was more about an identity for a brand. An irreverent, even gruff personality. A brand, a store, a chicken, you felt good about. *My chickens eat better than you do* an aggressive, go-fuck-yourself line Ed was famous for. An identity, not a strategy. A likeable, if scruffy personality. (Just like him.) And me as a consumer, would want to frequent the store or buy the chicken that spoke to you, to me, cleverly.

As I toiled unsuccessfully, I believed during that time

Back in the Star Again

I stood by as Ed catapulted Volvo into the American consciousness. A good time for imports. Side by side, as I sweated and stayed late and had a hard time pleasing him, he was writing ads for Volvo. For Perdue. *It goes from 60 to 0 in seconds flat. It takes a tough man to make a tender chicken.*

OK. So maybe they don't write 'em the way they used to. OK. So maybe they don't even hold up the way they used to. (They do.) But I am here and I am still trying to write these lines the way I learned 'em and the way I still want to write 'em. Recently, for Olay Regenerist, a chic drugstore brand of moisturizers, compared favorably, if not exactly, to cosmetic procedures. I wrote this line: *Some women nip and tuck. Others prefer the cutting edge.* A line with an attitude inspired by my time with Ed McCabe thirty-eight years ago.

I got fired from SMS for reasons I can only say have to do with my snide personality. My insecure anger, my impatience. But more about that later. And well, it takes two to tango. And to fire. I was maybe too much or maybe not enough. When you get fired in advertising, you never really know if it's you or if it's them or if it's just business. Or if it's whatever. I got fired. Not downsized. Fired. I was 27.

One last thing about Scali, McCabe, Sloves before we move on to the next. Marvin Sloves, the Merv Griffin look-alike head of account services, gay as a goose, used to come on to me in a subtle way. I was young and cute,

What I Do

I suppose (No. I was.) I couldn't handle the attention and I'm sure that may have been why I was fired, too. He had the oddest expression that I still don't quite get—"You'll be farting through velvet," he would say to me. And once, even said it in a crowded elevator. Can you imagine someone today in a corporate environment, even the big boss, especially the big boss, saying this to a young, vulnerable writer with an elevator full of witnesses?

Fired from Scali, I retreated for a few weeks to the Greek Islands. I was seven years into the biz and had saved some dough. It was a memorable vacation; I was able to put being fired behind me. As soon as I got back, I landed a job immediately at a small agency that specialized in fashion advertising. With a book of ads and a resume, or CV as they call it now, that bent towards fashion with Barney's, I got a job at Sacks & Rosen. I was hired for $40,000 a year (I asked for $45,000 but was knocked down once again) and given a large office with a slew of windows. I started working on small, precious print ads for accounts like Pierre Cardin Fragrance for Men in its iconic penis-shaped bottle. Ads for Yves Saint Laurent Rive Gauche, for Lady Manhattan Blouses. Cricketeer Suits. Mademoiselle Magazine. An art director there that I really liked, Dennis D'Amico (now gone from throat cancer, a big, angry talent dead by 50) said to me when we met: "You're Hy Abady? Gee, I thought you'd be so much older." I knew I had a name then, insecure as I may have been, and may always be, I was getting known for my work.

Sacks & Rosen lasted only a year and a half but it ignited in me a lifelong passion for fashion advertising. Barney's, at Scali, didn't really count. Ed insisted the Barney's ads be clever and conceptual. At Sacks, it was more superficial and…well, more about fashion. Every Sunday in the New York Times Magazine in those mid-70s, there were as many as three or four Sacks ads, small as that agency was, in a single issue. And all were mine, as I was the agency's sole writer.

There were ads for Salton, the company that made the Hot Tray that kept meals warm table side: *Women: Stand up for your right to sit down at dinner.* And a peanut butter maker: *Now you can make the stuff that sticks to the roof of your mouth under your own roof.* Nina Ricci was a client—the lovely L'Air du Temps perfume in the classic Lalique flacon with frosted glass doves as stopper. There was a decided elegance to the clients attracted to Lenny Sacks and his wife Harriet.

Lenny was the owner. Leonard Sacks. President, Account Guy. But more than that, a guy with an eye. Although he employed a head art director with lots of taste, Lenny was the last word in how all the ads would look and sound. He was a gifted marketer, believing that ads should be run over and over again thereby raking in media commission bucks without generating new ads and the cost of new plates for production. Lenny made out like the Frito Bandito with those media commissions.

Lenny was as tan as George Hamilton, with an oceanfront home in Westhampton Beach, a winter place in Boca Raton. He never worked a Friday. He chain-smoked and spit, like a baseball player, onto his plush, beige shag carpeting. His wife, Harriet, worked there as a stylist for the ads and she was the most glamorous woman I had ever met. Platinum blond, tan, too, chunky jewelry, the real thing. Trifari was a costume jewelry client (*The most extravagant $50 necklace ever made*) but she would only wear the real things except when the Trifari client visited the offices. Otherwise, it was Cartier and Bulgari and Harry Winston. High glamour, thin as Nan Kempner who, I think, was a friend. Perfume wafted away after her, as she left my office in her loose, flow-ey dresses, silk and linen and chiffon. In shades of earth tones and beiges. I would sit in her office, smoke cigarettes and look at portfolios of models considered for jobs. I remember the Rene Russo shoot for a Lady Manhattan blouse although I forget the line I wrote…

I didn't stay long, I got restless and impatient, and anxious to earn more—my salary stayed in the mid-40,000 range for that year and a half and I did get a bunch of more notice for some of the work. Oddly and mysteriously, I got a call from Money Magazine during that Sacks time.

Back in the Star Again

They wanted to interview me, a single guy, 27 years old and earning $45,000 a year. They wanted to know how I managed my money. A woman took me to lunch at the Palm, but I turned the idea of the story down. Was it so special? The things you choose and the things you choose not to choose.

I got lured away by more money but I'm still haunted by Lenny and Harriet. I dream about them often, thirty-five years later. I believe I thought of them as a set of parents, but much more elegant and sophisticated and thinner than my own. Them, with their chunky Lalique zigzag ashtrays, four of them anchoring down the corners of a gleaming glass and stainless steel coffee table in their enormous upper East Side apartment, beige and brown everywhere, like the office. And what they wore. And the intensity of their tans after a long Boca weekend in February.

The next job that lured me away with more money was a mistake but memorable just the same for more of a life-changing experience than the work. Let me say here and now how easy it was to get jobs then. With or without a headhunter. There were a handful of agencies that interested me, maybe a dozen, and I would just send my book to one of those places and get hired. Amazing. It helped, too, at the time, that I was young and, I guess, cheap to acquire. Today, not only are there no agencies that would fill my list of interesting places, but the business

What I Do

is so continually shrinking and no one seems to want to pay me my salary. Plus, I'm 62. The world's oldest, living copywriter—er, creative director. I remember when I was the youngest person in a meeting. Younger by a decade. Now, it's quite the reverse and you can subtract a decade or two from my age and then you'll find the next oldest person in the room.

But back to the tale.

The next agency was called Epstein, Raboy. Both Epstein and Raboy are dead now and the place was barely even alive then, but it was a place that introduced me to this place: Amagansett. They offered me $50,000 a year (although I didn't last a year) but it might have been a mistake to go because I missed the glamour of Sacks & Rosen right off and there wasn't much for me to work on. My partner, the art director I'll call Jeff (because his name was Jeff) had a Quaalude problem and walked into walls often. And Dick Raboy, the creative director/writer had a gambling and a food addiction. But Mitch Epstein came into my office one day and asked if I would be interested in sharing a rental house in Amagansett, a Frisbee toss from the ocean. I had never heard of Amagansett. I was a Jersey shore kind of guy with relatives in Bradley Beach and Deal. I didn't know from the Hamptons in 1977. But I agreed to take a drive out on a rainy April Saturday and I never left. That rental led to another rental at a different place. I had gotten fired from E/R in less than a year and I will get into that. But first, the one ad I liked that I did there but never got produced was for a Scotch named Swing. So named because it came in a bottle that, sort of, swung. It wouldn't tip over, it was meant to rest on a shelf in a boat, impossible to fall over. *Scotch and salt water* my headline. Picturing four people drinking scotch on a sailboat. It never got produced and I did get fired. But that line is, I think, indicative of my kind of one-liner. Ed McCabe inspired. Clever. It's these kinds of lines that has kept me employed lo these 42 years. Recently, as a nod to my roots, I wrote an ad for a facial cleansing wipe for Olay: *Become a woman of the cloth.*

OK, OK. The firing story. Epstein Raboy had a piece of Revlon as business and pretty new offices on Third Avenue and 49th Street, opposite Smith & Wollensky. Everything was new in the offices, somewhat custom designed for them. A lot of the offices sat empty and then there was news of lost business. There was little to do that fall, the fall after my first Amagansett summer, 1977. Dick Raboy came into my office one day that fall and said I was being let go because he didn't feel he should baby sit a $50,000 a year writer. I didn't know what he meant—I was a capable guy when given something to do. I think he didn't want to admit that they were not doing so well and I was friendly enough with the guy not to push it. Fired again, 29 years old. "Let's have lunch tomorrow and we'll discuss severance and the like," he said and I agreed to. It was mid-October and I had made up my mind that night, that because of the embarrassment and the suddenness of it—just the day before he fired me were we playing gin rummy, as we often did in the office since there was not much for any of us to do but play darts and cards (for money)—I made up my mind to ask to be paid until the end of the year. Two and a half months of severance.

We went to Smith & Wollensky for that farewell lunch. We ordered. Now, this Dick was really heavy. Obese, in fact, and like the Sackses, a chain-smoker, heck, we all were in those years, myself included. But he was really fat. Smith & Wollensky is a snazzy place, hushed for a steak house. Guys in suits, like all steak houses. We ordered drinks, we did that then at lunch. And I ordered what I still order in a steak house: chopped salad, filet mignon, butterflied and well-done with A.1., side of cottage fries and onion rings. I don't remember what Dick ordered, but it had to be that and more. Red wine came. "So, Hy," he started. "About the severance."

"Yeah, I was thinking…" I said, but then he interrupted me and said: "We've decided to give you until the end of this week." It was Tuesday.

"I was hoping till the end of the year!" I said. I was fired. I didn't have to be nice to the guy anymore.

He laughed. "End of the week is all we can do."

Back in the Star Again

The food arrives. Heaps of steaming platters of charred meats. Crisp, overflowing potatoes and onion rings. Two salads that could each feed four.

"That's your final offer?" I said, incredulous, as the plates were set down.

"That's it," he said, not looking at me, looking at the food.

I got up and left the table and walked straight out of the restaurant leaving him with all that food alone. Maybe that's what he wanted.

It wouldn't be the last time I'd be fired. But the very next job, come in a minute through a headhunter, was at a place called Benton & Bowles. This was a departure for me. This was not the creative type of place that had been all my roots so far. This was an agency known for packaged goods (Procter & Gamble!) and a different kind of advertising than what I was used to. But they were paying $50,000 a year and when you get fired, you want to prove that you're not a loser and you can easily get another job. I took it. On the Grape Nuts account. It would prove to be another mistake, an unhappy time—culturally, I felt I had lost my way and everything felt alien. It was saved by two things. I did get to work with an art director I had known at Doyle Dane—a nice guy who had been fired somewhere along the line, too, and found himself also in a place unfamiliar but he had children and a house in New Rochelle. (I was single with modest expenses and the 50 grand went a long

What I Do

way in 1977. I rented a house in Wainscott over that winter.) The second thing was I got my very first trip to LA, which I have grown to love having been there now, on many agencies nickels, maybe a hundred times. But this was my first time. And I was shooting a commercial for Grape Nuts with a Will Rogers-like Wilford Brimley. *"There's a real nice feeling in neighborhoods everywhere…"* the commercial started off. It was about how people are going back to nature, putting up vegetable gardens, eating healthily. The Grape Nuts strategy fit right into that. It was a nothing commercial, not funny, not clever. Homespun. And homespun was not my thing. But I got to LA and stayed in a swanky hotel—L'Hermitage, stunning and low-slung amid palms and bougainvillea, on an immaculate, sun-drenched, quiet boulevard in Beverly Hills. The producer of the spot from the agency played the piano every night at the bar atop the hotel. He'd play and sing show tunes. Like a seasoned, witty, Broadway celebrity. There were cocktails and the clear, starry sky of Southern California. It was all a bit slower, there, I felt that pace to be much slower than New York, at that time, and I remember coming across a Quaalude myself from a waiter at the hotel. I took it and liked LA even more.

But the job itself caused me problems. No less, I turned 30 in the middle of it and had a bit of a crisis. It was the one and only time I quit a job without another job, but

Back in the Star Again

I wasn't sleeping at nights and I was dreading going in every morning. For some reason, I got separated from the art director that I related to and was put on the Marine Midland Bank account with people I thought were drab and untalented. Sheepishly, nervously, I went into the head creative director's office one morning, white and shaking, looking like a person close to a breakdown. I told him I had to leave. He put his arm around my shoulder and, sympathetically, I believed, he understood.

"It's just not my thing," I said, trembling.

"I understand."

It was as though I was telling him I was too good for the place or the place was just too compromised for me. Maybe he wasn't all that sympathetic after all, but I was out of there and jobless once more.

That same headhunter who got me that last job suggested FREELANCE. It was a new concept in 1978, I didn't know any other copywriters doing it, but it sounded great to me. I didn't have to commit to a place, except for a day, or a week, or a month. I set my price at $250 a day and I was off to the races! It worked for me, I didn't have to play politics, something I would always be bad at, and I could be independent and pursue other writing interests. At that time, I wanted to be a lyricist. I had discovered the Broadway theatre and wanted to be Fred Ebb, who wrote the lyrics for *Chicago*, *Cabaret* and

What I Do

New York, New York. It was something I pursued during those two years of freelance, I even took piano lessons in case I wanted to compose, too, but those 'talents' and desires fell flat after I realized I was no good at that. What I was good at, and quick at, was those one-liners. I worked at places for a few days or a few months and pretty soon I was earning $500 a day, but, in the end, I felt a lack of commitment, a lack of client contact. Although I did get direct contact with a client who was a cousin of mine running a coffee business and did a series of three ads that won more awards. I had been building up a name by now, and since my name was unusual, people kind of remembered it. They thought I was Japanese or Muslim: Hya Badi? The ads were for Gillie's 1840 and this cousin of mine was really ahead of the curve with the coffee idea a good decade and a half before Starbucks. A coffee store that sold dried fruits and nuts. Soaps. Teas. These kinds of things. I really liked those small space ads I did at the time, me at either my most corniest or my most clever: *Our prunes aren't the only reason why we have so many regular customers.* And: *There are just as many fruits and nuts on the upper East Side as there are in the Village.* (this for a second location) and, well, this kind of thing. That was a high point, tuxedo on again at the New York Hilton. It won two pencils—one for first place small space ad (they ran in New York Magazine, in the front) and the other second place for best small space

Back in the Star Again

campaign. The awards themselves are two sided pencils, one for art, one for writing, get it? and they were heavy as Oscars. And they were delightful to win because there were all those hot-shots there, like the Oscars, handing them out. As odd footnote coincidence, it was Ed McCabe who had to hand me those two pencils from the podium, five years after he fired me.

But freelance was mostly like masturbating versus having sex. Not the real thing. Half the job, really. And as I was using the exact same brain cells to come up with the lines whether I was staff or freelance, there was no follow through. No client meetings. No finished proofs. I liked that part of the business, too, I found out during that lucrative freelance period. I was ready to dip back into the real world of the business of advertising full-on commitment.

DKG was another one of what they called 'boutique' agencies. Scali was one. There were a few hot-shit New York agencies that scorned the likes of big business: Volvo vs. GM a good example, their clients were usually underdogs looking to make an impact with a lesser advertising budget. Their accounts were Aamco Transmissions (no, they didn't come up with the double-A horn-honk pnemonic, that was at another agency, earlier) Ricoh Cameras, the Tropicana Hotel in Atlantic City, Remington Shavers, and others of that ilk. Toshiba electronic, another account—in fact, I did a radio commercial, where I did get to write lyrics at last.

What I Do

And the "jingle" was sung by none other than Luther Vandross, just before he hit it big, recorded for me, via a music producer. A nice moment, DKG. Not filled with the biggest names, more mid-tier brands and scrappy entrepreneurial guys who were looking for a leg up. DKG did some very clever and smart ads, not the top of the heap at the time, but just right, I felt. Back to my roots.

And it would be a wonderful job for me in those early '80s. They paid me well. I had a spiffy, rectangular office, 36 stories up in the Time/Life Building opposite Radio City Music Hall. There was the US Steak House in the lobby, a Restaurants Associates place and there was another restaurant on the top floor. Dizzying, everything was in those years. I bought my house in Amagansett in the middle of that job and won my first Clio. Having really been known as a print person primarily, DKG gave me a lot of TV experience, most memorable of all was the work I did for Aamco Transmissions. You may not remember the work, but when I was involved with it I thought it was the best time with daring, fun work, and trips to Chicago and lots of LA. We hired this director, a real zany character, straight out of the Marx Brothers or Jacques Tati. His name was Joe Sedelmeier and he was based in Chicago and made a huge name for himself for, among other things, directing Clara Peller in *Where's The Beef* for Wendy's and doing the even more brilliant

Fast Talking Man for Federal Express. Federal Express was what really put him on the comedic map. He directed dozens of hilarious, deadpan commercials for FedEx, using not so much actors as real people that he would tell them precisely how to read the lines. "Repeat after me. No, exactly this way!" Abusive, but hilarious. And he got exactly the readings he wanted out of them. Aamco was a less successful version for Sedelmeier than FedEx was, FedEx was a new, hot emergent company. A new idea, the brainchild of another entrepreneur, Fred Smith. All packages went to Memphis, the hub, even if they were being sent around the block in the Bronx. It spawned an industry. And Joe Sedelmeier, with the creative work from an agency I was soon to work for (keep reading) began it all and made it happen. The FedEx work is still clever today, now coming from BBDO. Funny how certain clients, no matter what agency they wind up switching to, maintain a high level of creativity. FedEx is a good example. Volkswagen, another. And, funny, I can't think of too many others.

But I skip around.

Joe Sedelmeier shot Aamco and I got to put on a tuxedo again, now upgraded with silver lurex thread in the black velvet jacket, subtle but striking at the same time. That night, I won two Clios for my work on Aamco. And they were funny, out-there spots, with chimpanzees banging on transmissions and appliances breaking down before the warranties expire. (Does anyone remember?) Oh, well. They were memorable at the time. And I was making the most money I'd ever made, freelance having upped my ante to the hundred thou mark and I went even beyond that at DKG. They paid me in expenses and, somehow, off the books. Clever bookkeeping. Jewish accountant. Like my ads. Clever enough to allow me to afford $190,000 for a house a block from the ocean in Amagansett that I live in and love to this day.

(Another story.)

There was a lot to be said for DKG. Interestingly enough, as happens to agencies, especially if you stick around long enough and I was there for about four years, the names change. And when DKG changed its name to reflect the new partners at the top, they ran an ad in trade journals to announce their new name. The ad read: *DKG. A name to forget.* (I didn't write it.) The new agency was called Calet, Hirsch, Kurnit & Spector. Law-firm-ish. And with that forgettable new name they never reached the small heights that DKG did. But, truth be told, those years, those early '80s, was when advertising as I knew it from my youth, started falling off its cliff.

At DKG, I attended my first focus group to get consumers reaction to advertising ideas. The business would never be the same again. Granted, those early focus groups, for Ricoh

Back in the Star Again

cameras, was in LA and I was with the boss and we got to frequent the chic Chianti restaurant on Melrose and have Mexican at Lucy's El Adobe, but it was the beginning of the end. Planners also came into the picture during that period, and they seem here to stay—still one more layer diluting the creative process. Clients were now MBAs. Business people who looked at bottom lines vs. headlines. Frank Perdue and Fred Pressman (of Barney's) and Fred Smith (of Federal Express) were the exceptions. Now, the people who judged the advertising were somehow of a different breed than what I grew up with during that now golden and mad men age. They didn't really know how to recognize creative work, they were more involved in test results and the always elusive and impossible to ascertain idea of what sells.

What sells? Here's my take on what sells. What sells is when you feel good about a product, when you appreciate the messages they throw out there on the tube and in the mags. When you get that visceral feeling, that feel-good feeling about a brand, about a company. Think Apple. Think Volkswagen again. I switched from Diet Pepsi to Diet Coke, personally, and as a consumer and not just an ad guy, when I saw that Diet Coke commercial sometime in those changing '80s, that featured a construction guy taking off his shirt and having a Diet Coke while three women from an office above ogled him in a clever turnaround. Consciously, for me, I decided to support that brand and make that crucial switch. Conscious, for me. Unconscious for most other people not in the business but bombarded by images and forced to make choices.

There. I said it.

Now, on with the career. (We're midway there, at this point.)

DKG/Calet Hirsh, whatever, fired me one morning but hired me back that same afternoon for reasons too confusing and emotional on the part of Peter Hirsh (now dead) to relate. No matter. A short while after that I landed what I thought was again, the dream job, at the most sophisticated boutique of the era. Ally & Gargano. And was I vindicated. Fuck you, whatever your name to forget or remember is or was. I've scored the job of the decade and, without looking back, I left. For the first time in my career, I left for a lateral salary move—in fact, I think it was even less that what I was making for the first time, but I thought it a wise career move. After four years at the name to forget and some more notice for the work on Aamco, I was ready to move, never forgetting that they fired me, even if it only was for a couple of hours.

Now, remember back some pages my four-day job at Carl Ally some twelve years earlier? Well, that agency had changed its name to Ally & Gargano, and in those intervening years, they became the most interesting agency in New York. More like an architectural firm, serious and solemn, no laughter in the halls, no barber chairs in the offices, Ally & Gargano was hushed and brilliant and I was so very pleased with myself that I landed a job there. With a corner office, no less—well, half a corner in the newly built Crystal Pavillion on 3rd Avenue and 49th Street, above Smith & Wollensky. And right across the street from Scali and Epstein Raboy, two agencies I had been fired from in the distant 1970s. But wait. I was to be fired from Ally & Gargano, too, in two years time, and still, when I walk down that block in New York, I sometimes feel the buildings will fall down on me and finish me altogether.

It hasn't happened. Yet.

But I get ahead of myself. The two years at Ally & Gargano were extraordinary. I felt like I was finally in the right place, even if it was slightly the wrong time. A bit late in their fabulousness. Everything was changing in those mid-80s. Agencies were buying up other agencies and holding companies were buying up the merged results. But it was the last absolute second of creativity and Ally & Gargano was doing a lot of the work to keep that heritage alive. I was thrilled to be there, working amongst the last giants I knew who were doing the work, day to day, year by year, traveling first class to LA, staying at the Beverly Hills Hotel. I was shooting Polaroid there (funny, I worked on Polaroid at the very beginning of my career and found it stifling, now I was working on it again just as the technology was starting to fade) and renting an

What I Do

aqua Alfa Romeo spider—gosh, did that happen? But even more spectacular was the two trips to Paris to shoot Polaroid commercials by the Eiffel Tower. How that happened is thusly: Polaroid, just at the beginning of their demise, felt the strategy was that this was the camera that made sure you got the once-in-a-lifetime shot. Long before one-hour photo, more than a decade before digital, Polaroid, at that moment, preyed on the idea that you can go to Paris and take pictures but until you got home, you never knew if you got the shot. With a Polaroid, at the Eiffel Tower, you knew in 60 seconds if you got the shot. Crazy, now, looking back, but it got me to Paris. And twice, because the first time we went, a crew of some twenty of us, couldn't get to shoot because it rained every day for ten days in late March. We spent afternoons in cafes and bistros, drinking wine, waiting for the sun to come out. It didn't We left, and returned a month later, ten more days at the excruciatingly elegant Hotel de Crillon, and got the shots and got the spot and it was a lackluster commercial but I had foie gras and ate at Guy Savoy and thought I was really living the life. And I was. But that was to come crashing back down to Earth and further still, down to hell, some months later.

In the fall of 1985, a year and a half into my deliriously happy job at Ally—another short form name, but a very sophisticated place, and all I ever wanted in an agency,

Back in the Star Again

I seemed to have sabotaged it all. Unknowingly.

They had the Saab account. In full support of my appreciation of being an employee of Ally, I decided to lease a Saab, a decidedly un-sexy Swedish car. I had been driving a sexy black Fiat Spider convertible that was, the way of Italian cars, breaking down weekly. I wanted a Saab to show my solidarity and I got one from an upper West Side dealership called Zumbach Motors, now, like Ally & Gargano, and Saab itself, gone. It was a pretty French blue and had a hatchback and was touted as safe, reliable, indestructible. I picked up this highly dependable car on a Wednesday before Thanksgiving and was prepared to drive it out to the Hamptons for a dinner party I was hosting the next day for 20 people. Driving out with a friend, Sedelmeier's rep and producer, a gorgeous, glamorous woman named Mason. She brought champagne for the maiden, in fact, voyage in the Saab and we drank some of it on the way out.

It was raining, damp and cool for late November. The car seemed fine 90 miles into the trip, another ten miles to home, when it started to buck and to wheeze. At a red light in Southampton, it wouldn't start. Then it did. Then it wouldn't. Just before entering Amagansett, the car dropped dead. Not 100 miles on the odometer and it just wouldn't go any further. I was crazed, to say the least, I still had to shop for this Thanksgiving dinner in 24 hours time, had to pick people up from the train and the bus. Had to pretend, that a car I spent upwards of $25,000 for, granted, a lease, but still, was now stuck on the side of the road outside of Hren's Nursery—the trees and shrubs kind, a couple of miles from my weekend home.

Somehow, by cabs, I guess, I was so enraged by this episode that I blacked out, it all worked out and the party was a success, as the Saab 900 S sat in the rain, plastered with gold and red and yellow leaves at the side of Montauk Highway. On that Friday after Thanksgiving, I called Zumbach. They left outgoing messages that they were closed, but press one for a person. That person, was not helpful. "Sir," that person said. "It's the Friday after Thanksgiving. There is no service today. Call back Monday." And, click.

My rage boiled up further. But without a car, in a part of town where one needs a car, I called other Saab dealerships all over Long Island and finally got to a sympathetic person somewhere in Smithtown. That person, that lovely dealership, arranged to have that wretched Saab, stuck on the side of the road, picked up at no expense to me and looked after by those Smithtowners.

A few days later, back in New York, the anger mostly subsiding, I was told the car was ready to be picked up. Good as new. As it was new. And I took the LIRR to get to it and drove it back to New York, it performing like a Saab is supposed to perform—smooth and reliable.

But, well, as a writer, as a naïve person, somehow at this

point eighteen years into my illustrious, ding-dong, back and forth career, I decided to alert these Saab people about this distressing experience. I contacted the head account guy to get the name of the head client and proceeded to write him (that would be a Bob Sinclair, who I heard died recently) an angry 3-page letter. Oh, it was fiery, all right. I wrote the hell out of it. Getting into how awful the treatment from Zumbach was. Letting them know how wonderful Smithtown was.

Vitriolic. That's the word for the letter. With a glass of Beaujolais Nouveau—this was the start of that fading phenom, I crafted this very written letter that I'm sure I saved somewhere in my archives of nonsense. I was impressed with how I pulled it all together.

I was impressed. No one else was. In fact, what would you call the opposite of impressed? Depressed?

So—and this gets a little hard to write—the outcome of the letter, well...the head account director, a stiff suit type named Dennis Something-Or-Other came into my pie-wedge-shaped corner office one dreary December day and asked, incredulously: *"Did you send a letter to Robert Sinclair? About your Saab?!"* Incredulous, that look, I will never forget, on his face. I was perplexed. I believed I was innocent.

Innocent!

"Well, Amil has gotten wind of this letter of yours," he said. *This letter of yours.* Like it was a bomb. Which, it turned out to be.

"Well, the car really did break down. Died on me," I said, nervously. "With less than 100 miles on the odometer!" I continued." It was outrageous the fact that they wouldn't, they couldn't..." but my words did trail off, as I sensed, no, this was not the PC thing to do.

"Amil will get in touch with you and tell you how he feels about your...er, letter."

That bomb!

And now, I was on total edge, waiting, wondering, what the reaction would be. It came quickly

One anxious morning, I got a notification, a (pink) "While You Were Out" hard copy note, something an assistant wrote out by hand, long before voice mail and texting and what have you: Amil Gargano called. Would like to see you, checked in its appropriate pink box.

Well, he saw me, all right. Ice-cold and irritated beyond belief, he faced me. "I will deal with this and you after the holidays, Hy," he said, stern as a headmaster at a teen-age boys prep school.

And boy, did he.

I got fired in January. "Cutbacks and, sorry," he said. "The loss of Polaroid and all..." he said.

Bullshit, as far as I was concerned.

"You fired me because of that letter, didn't you," I courageously ventured. I mean, what was I to lose at this

Back in the Star Again

point, already fired, what the fuck?!

"It had nothing to do with that," he insisted, cold as an ice cube.

Insisting that that was the reason, I ended it with: "Well, at least I know my writing had an impact!"

He couldn't suppress a huge laugh with that.

And I left.

And I headed for Key West, wounded, confused, depressed.

In Key West, kind of like Greece a couple of firings before, licking my wounds with martinis at noon—there's that *Mad Men* connection again, except now I was again an out of work writer in Key West. Imagining my future as a restaurant critic, a theatre reviewer, within the supporting writer arms and palms of Key West.

Strange, though. Though I rented a romantic second story conch house in Old Town, I had an answering machine. Perhaps the only person on Key West with an answering machine, this, 1986, early in the year. I took a train from Penn Station to Miami, loaded with my essentials, my stuff, and, still, an enormous electric typewriter. Then, a Greyhound bus from Miami to Key West, just for the experience of it. (It wasn't worth it.)

So. The answering machine. Midst those drunk and then napped and then hung over Key West afternoons, I got a message from the famous Judy Wald, headhunter extraordinaire, the real old school, old as Zsa Zsa Gabor and as glamorous and face-lifted.

"There's a job at Foote Cone Belding I think you'd be perfect for." "Bleep!"

I called back and a week later I was back in New York, my three-month lease and paid in full in Key West, surrendered after less than three weeks in that second story.

But I was home. And I was employed again. Not forgotten.

Foote, Cone, however, not the place once again that would hold me for long.

Their offices, on Park Avenue and 40th Street, a spanking new building, again, angles and glass and steel. My office, a big fat corner this time, was separated from other offices with plants. Waist-high plants. Not exactly cubicles as we've come to know them today. Just horizontal, horticultural separations and quite odd.

A friend, a fellow compatriot copywriter came to visit me one afternoon. He knew I was miserable at this job.

"Well, at least you have a corner plant," he said and that made me laugh. But the job overall made me cry, so confused again, like Benton & Bowles now almost ten years ago.

I called Jerry Della Femina.

I got a new job. Thank you, Jerry, for enfolding me back to my roots. Those smaller agencies, clever, creative joints that made me feel, always, like I was a star.

Back in the Star Again

Now we're getting to the later '80s here in the story. Jerry hired me at a respectable 150 thou in 1986. Jerry Della Femina will always be for me a larger than life person. Funnier than anyone I've ever known. Loved to drink. Loved to smoke pot. Loved to laugh. And we would all laugh along with Jerry as he supplied another very social atmosphere, margarita lunches during snow days. Fun, fun, fun. And a fair amount of work that was, although not at the peak of his crowning moment—the '70s his real time with Eyewitness News and Pretty Feet and various other obscure accounts that made the awards books and gave him an enormous name as he also managed the classic tale of his fun adventures in advertising: *From Those Wonderful Folks Who Gave You Pearl Harbor* yes, a classic, Jerry also known for the line: *advertising is the most fun you can have with your clothes on*, and I hear that he is a consultant on *Mad Men* to authenticate its authenticity.

But that, too, is another story.

My four years at Jerry's place were somewhat turbulent, but the pot helped. He got sold and the name changed half a dozen times—these were the times when advertising really came into its own as something other than entrepreneurship, more like holding companies, and Jerry succumbed to sales and got himself a major, beachfront East Hampton home in the interim. Unpretentious though, Mr. Della Femina. With his restaurant and his column in his daughter's newspaper. And his hilarity.

He fired me, too. Well, not him, exactly, his dutiful white-haired and faux-famous creative director, Jim Durfee.

Crazy how things wind up. Jim Durfee was also at Carl Ally, Inc. that job I had in early 1972 for four days. I had to interview with him as well as Amil Gargano, yes the same from Ally & Gargano, also fired by. Durfee was there at Carl Ally—are you able to keep up? And then he wound up being the guy who fired me in 1990 at Della Femina. I still don't know why except it's always couched in loss of business.

Begin anew! As always, as again. Hymo. Never say die, never want to be over with.

I got a call about some freelance at Wells, Rich Greene. To work on the Chase Manhattan Bank account. I was pulling in big day bucks at that job and after a few months of day-to-day dough, they asked me if I wanted to join the staff. (I shouldn't have.) So, after some careful negotiations, I was able to get $200,000 a year out of them. I shouldn't have. Although I met an art director there who would turn out to be a lifelong friend, that agency was not that agency that it once was. Mary Wells, an early idol of mine, was long gone. Charlie Moss, the executive creative director seemed less interested these days than in his heydays. And the new day-to-day creative director was some nobody with a swooping mink coat whose name was also Mary but bore

Back in the Star Again

no resemblance to what that agency was in the 1970s.

And, after a turbulent year of disrespect and boozy lunches that left me cranky and disillusioned, I got fired once again. Early 1992. I remember a dinner I had with a few friends the night I got fired. I stood up at the table in the West Village, held up a glass of wine and said, so loud it scared neighboring diners: "I will never get fired from this business again!" And I haven't. So far.

Next stop was another time off, this time six months off, once again to try to figure out the love/hate of it all, refusing offers and there were some, even refusing freelance. I needed the six months to chill even before that reference to retreating was coined.

Six months later, I did get a call from another creative boutique creative director. Strangely, they had the Saab account—I never did work on Saab at Ally, just got fired because of it, and now, comes around, comes around, I was asked to help out on that account. I dipped back in, said yes, and managed to write a headline for a Saab poster that, once again, put me in a small spotlight as it won an Obie award for best outdoor poster of 1992. The line on that poster is irrelevant today, but at the time... *Why settle for factory air?* I wrote. The visual a spanking white Saab 900 S convertible (it was the hardtop that got me fired) and the freaking poster ran right outside the Queens Midtown Tunnel on one's way to the Hamptons on the Long Island

Expressway. I would see it outside my windshield and think: I am not over with yet.

That period of freelance lasted awhile. I went to Backer Spielvogel Bates for a couple of forgettable years on M&Ms and Belmont Park. I wound up back for another couple of years at Ammirati & Puris, an offshoot of my earlier Scali, Ally types of places and worked with one of my favorite people ever in advertising—the lovely Helayne Spivak, funny, Jewish. (Google her and see all she's done.)

I did some wonderful work at Ammirati, but, alas, I was a freelancer. A day worker, not any more glamorous than the woman who cleaned my apartment by the day. Sometimes, when you freelance, you are looked upon as a bit of a loser. Like you can't get a full-time job and you can be let go without the slightest sense of a lawsuit and at any given moment. Fired every Friday is how someone once put it. Although I felt like a bit of a loser, I wound up doing some really good work for Cellular One, the precursor to ATT Wireless. *Open an office in the Holland Tunnel,* I wrote when the service was possible there. *Now it even works underwater,* I wrote about service in the Lincoln Tunnel. *Introducing the world's longest phone booth,* I wrote, about service there, too. Notable, but a day worker loser. And two years later, they couldn't afford to pay me anymore.

Moving on. But with some regret. Loser-ish as a freelancer can be, hello second citizen, no Christmas party invites, no high-level meetings, no health benefits, no respect, Ammirati was a nod, here in the mid-90s, to what used to be for me. Clever, old-school creative directors. Guys and women who grew up wherein I grew up, although they wound up richer and more famous, but we shared that same sensibility. Ralph Ammirati, the Italian art director that worked with Ed McCabe at that mentioned-over-and-over Ally agency, the agency that dogged me for decades, was famous in the in-crowd of the business for the work he did for Cinzano with Ed and let me digress back to the 1960s and those inspiring ads they did including one with the longest, intentionally rambling headline: *Cinzano ashtrays are only ashtrays. But Cinzano candlesticks are also vermouth.* I love the confident change of tense at the end of that line. Of course, it's dated—do they even make Cinzano anymore? But at the time, it worked because Cinzano ashtrays, when you could smoke in a restaurant and that bulb-shaped Cinzano bottle were candlesticks all over the Village and everywhere else.

But enough about Ed and Ralph and all these guys long out of the business now.

Me, like Sondheim says: I'm still here. For now.

Although the brief period post Ammirati, I faltered and felt, once again, that the business had forgotten me. But, you know, as you write something like this, as you evaluate and assess a career, a career as long and as varied as mine

What I Do

has been, there is no doubt that there will be ups and downs. The period right after Helayne and Ralph and Martin Puris—he said the phrase I overheard one day when the guys at the top were signing the deal to sell to Lintas (for a bunch of millions for each of them): *Don't Look Back*, not a headline, but something Martin said. There is no looking back in a business that changes every year. Don't look back. Well, there wouldn't be this story if I didn't, or couldn't, or wouldn't look back.

1996. More freelance. My rate sits steady at $1,000 a day, but sometimes, I can charge by the project and then, it escalates into stratospheric heights. Like, I would charge $7,500 for a tagline, or $10,000 for a campaign, and since now, so quick, those tag lines and campaigns could be done in a few hours.

You do the math. (I hate that expression.)

And then, sometime in 1997, I got a call from Sacks & Rosen! Another retread, another blast from the past, another mistake.

But I am a sentimental guy, if nothing but an extremely sentimental guy, and when I got the call from Sacks—now in the hands of the son of Sacks, a handsome guy named Andrew with not the style or the sense of the father, or the mother, I jumped at the chance. Now, back there some twenty-odd years later, it was not nearly the same.

I didn't have the big office with the plaid carpeting. The

mother was gone. The father was nowhere to be seen, but would be on speaker phone, like Big Brother here and there in the son's office, the same office the father used to smoke in and spit in.

But everything had changed. Still, I did jump at the chance because I sold Andrew a bill of goods that I believed to be absolutely true: I can help you grow! I can bring in new business! I am more than a writer, I am a seasoned advertising guy! at the peak of my powers, and I will bring in more fashion accounts than you can shake a shtick at.

Andrew was interested in me, but, in the end, he wanted to be the Big Kahuna. (Who doesn't?) And I never get the idea that I can be intimidating, or I can be something that nobody really wants. A lot of advertising people want to be IT. They really don't want any help from anybody else. We are all full of ourselves, aren't we?

Anyway, I am. Anyway, I was, as I joined Sacks & Rosen for the second time. It's funny. I went back to Doyle Dane twice, back to Ally twice and now, back again to what was a fun and inspiring job the first time around. But it was not lovelier the second time around. Sacks fils was a control freak. Not talented in any way I could see, except he played, I heard, a mean game of golf and cemented client relationships on the golf course if not with the advertising. Lackluster, the work done for Larson-Juhl Frames, Starck Carpet and Woodbury Commons. Interesting that thirty

What I Do

years later Sacks & Rosen (Rosen long gone, but the superstition was to keep the name intact from its glory, New York Times Magazine full-of-ads days) still attracted the same kind of fashion-ey accounts.

The job—another low point, was a cross between freelance and staff. Though, once again, like before, I was the only writer there. They could or would only pay me for three days a week. And, I repeat, a low point at $800 a day. But off the books and I could do my own advantageous tax structuring, and, good, too, was the fact that I could spend my other two days doing my other writing. Or other freelance. It was a bit of a disaster. *Everyone thinks they're a writer*, the writing is the easiest thing to criticize and amend and want to do. Art direction, I discover in the end, although a job requiring more hours, more office time, more knowledge of things now like Quark and Photoshop and Flash etc. is more mystifying than writing. Andrew wanted to write, heck, everyone wants to write, and rewrite my lines. Clients want to get into the act, too. A disaster. Six months later, the lackluster Andrew, the hopefully good golfer, let me go. As I said, a low point. Now, pushing 50 (that's 150 in copywriting years) and out of work again. Luckily, I have another career as a writer, and here it is, you are looking straight at it—I am published also with a short story here and there, and, thankfully, the Star does like my writing…but guess how

Back in the Star Again

much I make a day with these outside of advertising ventures? $0 a day. Which translates to $0 a year. It's advertising that pays the big bucks and there I was again, as 1997 drew to a close, earning $0 a day in advertising.

But I had another epiphany. With all the ups and downs, the awards, the staff, the freelance, the firings, with all my enthusiasm and my belief that I can bring in business, I decided to venture out on my own. Nope, not a freelancer no more, not a staff person—as it happened, freelance work exploded in the 1990s; I look back as one of the pioneers of that genre. I freelanced in the 1970s for fuck sake, and turned to it again in the '90s, turned to it always, really, when I felt down and out, turned to it when I was disappointed and confused and angry. I decided to head to a different direction. Nope, not freelance. I had some money saved and my 401Ks were doing fine, no, not Greece again, no, not Key West. I decided to invest $100,000 in myself. I worked it all out in my head. I had a plan. No longer beholding or a slave or a disrespected day worker. I was going to open up my own shop! Hy Abady, Inc—has a nice ring to it (if you could pronounce it properly) wouldn't you say? I was going to find myself a small office, hire myself a cute assistant, and not have to deal with politics or headhunters or answer to anyone but myself. Fuck. I have earned this time and this idea. 1998 marked thirty years as a solid, if slightly sloppy, professional. I was ready for my new next thing, ready for my close-up.

One February morning, focused on my future, I set out with a downtown commercial real estate broker to look for space. Downtown space, I was very interested in the emergent meat-packing district as the perfect new spot for me and that cute assistant. But, as all the signs of those times indicated, there was a minimum of 10,000 square feet required for rent. I was looking at, well, for my meager one hundred thou to last me a year, maybe 500 square feet. Plus, I had to pay that cute assistant. The broker suggested I look into Chelsea Piers and that sounded interesting enough. Perhaps a small room there, with a water view, to get me started. Sounded good. And I saw a room there one afternoon and it seemed rather perfect. I nodded to her, yes, this might very well do, when my cell phone rang.

Ring of destiny, as it were.

It was Tod Seisser—one 'd' Tod. Tod. Odd Tod, Od Tod? a guy I worked with at Backer, Spielvogel, Bates (once known as Ted Bates, then known as Backer, now, like so many of the places I have worked for, gone). He was an intense art director, one of those art directors I've grown to be uncomfortable with. One of those art directors who fancies himself a writer (everyone's a writer), this one I had worked with in 1993 on one of the accounts I had the least feel for: Miller Lite Beer.

Back in the Star Again

I don't drink beer. I hate beer. You know, I've come to know for myself—the best work I do is for the products I have a feel for even if I've never replaced a transmission at Aamco. But all the fashion stuff, the cute VW beetle, the luxury goods at Sacks and elsewhere, are things I know or aspire to. Bentley Motor Cars, Hasselblad Cameras, I like luxury. Thing is, you really have to have a feel for the products you work on to make it believable.

Tod Seisser was the newly appointed executive creative director at Saatchi & Saatchi—a million-dollar-a-year-plus post he acquired no doubt due to the humorous work he had done at Ammirati & Puris on Philip's Milk of Magnesia. Remember Raymond and Maureen? That elderly African-American couple that made constipation funny? Tod had a name in the '90s, he came up at places like Della Femina and, still one more defunct agency now: Levine, Huntley, Schmidt, Plapler and Beaver. There was an old joke about the length of that agency's name—the telephone operator answers the phone and says: "Good morning, Levine, Huntley, Schmidt, Plapler and Beaver. Good afternoon." Perhaps too much obscure information here, but safe to say that Tod Seisser was perhaps the Hy Abady of the '90s as I was the Hy Abady of the '70s. Award-winning, respected, but the slight difference with him was he won recognition for packaged goods and Saatchi & Saatchi was all about packaged

What I Do

goods: Procter & Gamble, General Mills and Johnson & Johnson. Right there, he called, as I was seriously contemplating my small and precious place in advertising history with two small rooms and a water view if you stuck your head out of the men's room window at Chelsea Piers, the phone rang.

"Hello, Hy?" Tod said. Destiny. "As you may have heard, I'm the new creative director at Saatchi," he said, humbly, although humbly is said tongue in cheek as no one is humble in advertising—all creatives are full of themselves, myself included, if maybe less so. "And, we've just been awarded the Oil of Olay account from Wells, Rich, Greene"—as an aside, this is another agency which has also imploded—Ha! I thought. Another agency that fired me out of business. Cool. Ally, Scali, Epstein Raboy, Benton & Bowles, Backer, all of them gone. Ha! And good riddance!

"Sure, Tod, I had heard you snagged that job," I said, although I hadn't heard. You learn to lie in advertising. That's what advertising is. Lies. White ones and otherwise lies.

"So, I was wondering. If you're still in the freelance market, and you, with your extensive fashion and beauty experience—" another empty advertising truth, like lies, butter them up if you what to get something out of them.

"Well, since we have no writers for the account and since you're so good at that, just wondering, would you be interested in coming in to freelance on that account

Back in the Star Again

for a short while until we can staff it up, properly?"

The real estate agent stood there, annoyed, tapping her foot, looking at her watch.

Destiny.

"Sure, Tod", no extra d. "Why, not?" I said and thought, no harm in doing a few days, or even a few weeks—I never really knew where freelance by the day would turn into. I would turn 50 in two months time, and even if it lasted two months time, fine. I could still contemplate my new business model in that time and make a few bucks while at it.

Now, here's the best thing: As usually happens with agencies, when they want you, they want you immediately. And Tod wanted me immediately, not only for Oil of Olay but for an obscure Procter shampoo account, he said, that he was having trouble cracking. Physique, the brand. I told him I had a trip planned, a long President's Day weekend jaunt to St. Bart's—which I couldn't cancel. And, why would I? Why should I? I mean, this was freelance (again) nothing permanent or connected to, nothing career-making, just money, just freelance, something in between, nothing that couldn't wait, but still there at Chelsea Piers, the agent still tapping, he said: "I don't want to insult you, Hy, of course, I know what you are capable of doing, but if you wouldn't mind showing your work to Beverly Okada, the creative director on (Oil of) Olay and Physique, so she can be just as

What I Do

impressed with what you do as I am…"

(Lies.)

So I send my work to Beverly Okada, the gentle but firm but wonderful woman who I still work for twelve years later. And she approves. Crazy how things work—in advertising and elsewhere and everywhere, in fact, but they said they needed the Physique work immediately. It was then, my $1,500 a day rate secured, that I said I was leaving for my short vacation and they wondered: could I fax them scripts from wherever I was going? At $1,500 a day?!

"Sure," I said. And so, I would fax them scripts, shampoo scripts I'd write on the gorgeous, exclusive beaches of St. Bart's and this: this is the high life or the Hy life, if you will, that the business owed me afer the disappointment of son of Sacks (and all the others). Earning $1,500 a day, faxing these scripts, and even in the stratospheric expensiveness of St. Bart's, I was ahead of the game. And, it seemed, again, still ahead of me. Not forgotten, nope, not me. On top of it, even if it was Saatchi & Saatchi wanting me now. Heck, I was nearing 50…did I mention that? And most guys my age, even as faux-famous as I am, were discarded and over with as an IBM Selectric typewriter.

Yet, somehow, somewhy and probably because this was all I knew, this was all I ever wanted…

I will digress a moment here, please allow me this sentimentality, but there was a time, back before my first job, while still living in Brooklyn, I drove my mother's 1962 baby blue Pontiac Bonneville into Manhattan one navy blue night, late, and parked on Madison Avenue and 50th Street, got out of the car, looked up and down the Avenue and said to myself and also aloud: *someday, I will own this street.*

That is true. It truly is. And although I don't own it by any means, and though I never rose to the heights of those aforementioned idols of mine, I hung in there, through thick and thin and everythin in between, and I'm still here. Or there. Or somewhere.

Saatchi & Saatchi.

Maurice and Charles, the Saatchi brothers, are long gone from there. One married Josephine Hart, she who wote the excellent novel "Damage" turned into a terrific movie with Jeremy Irons and Juliette Binoche, then divorced her and married the very sexy chef and cookbook writer, Nigella Lawson, the other Charles, or was it Charles with those wives? No matter. Google them, those Saatchis were very famous in advertising long after Ed and Carl and Bernbach. Brits who did wonderful work for British Airways in the 1980s when London was the center of the creative advertising universe. Cities come in creative spurts—Minneapolis of all places once hot thanks to Fallon, McElligott, Rice, also late '80s. Seattle big with Weiden and Kennedy, San Fran on the map with Chiat Day and Goodby, Silverstein. But, in 1998,

What I Do

with that silver and grey birthday cake building on Hudson and Houston, NYC, built in those faded 1980s still bearing their names although they are long gone and now respected art collectors with the Saatchi gallery in London their thing, discovering the likes of Damien Hirst and who-have-you.

(Boy, do I digress. But just to make it all interesting, I hope.)

Here's the relevant to the story thing—Saatchi & Saatchi, the agency that gobbled up Dancer, Fitzgerald, Sample and Compton and perhaps another stodgy, stuffy agency or two in those changing times of advertising in those long-gone 1980s, would be a place I would never consider working at (unless I was fired and in need of a job to not feel over with) Saatchi & Saatchi, with its opposite of creative driven accounts, like…well, Procter & Gamble, was a place I would have scoffed at and sniffed at in my heyday, in my tuxedo nights. Who, me? Saatchi & Saatchi? Packaged goods? Test commercials? Oh, no. Not me. I was the ultimate snob with my Doyle Dane Bernbach pedigree, my Allys and my Scalis and even my DKGs. But guess what? Saatchi & Saatchi and Beverly Okada and Oil of Olay, eventually, Olay, with its lack of awards and its decidedly dowdiness would become the best job I have ever had.

Crazy, right? Go know. I mean, who knows what anything will turn out to be, but what Saatchi turns out to be, Olay, now that I am past 60 (180 in copywriting years) I look back on all of it and maybe Olay and Saatchi is really what it's all about. Business results. Selling products. Not winning awards, not wearing tuxedos at awards functions, agencies that rise like rockets, then explode and fizzle and disintegrate.

Oil of Olay, when I first started at Saatchi as Physique faded like a fart, was a small obscure brand. Exotic and mysterious and 'my grandmother used that!' This pink beauty fluid in a glass bottle with a black cap and label and logo of an outlined, abstract woman's face. Procter bought the brand as it is wont to do. Procter, of Pringles and Pampers and Tide and Charmin and Bounty and every single other thing that sits in everyone's home all over the world. Procter bought Oil of Olay with its single iconic pink cream back in the early '90s, and turned it into what it's most famous for—soaps (Ivory, Camay, Safeguard). What started in that glass bottle is now soap, bodywash, body lotion and a whole slew of moisturizing sub-brands. And I was there and still am there as the senior copywriter/creative director of record.

That freelance job that was supposed to be brief, back in February of 1998, turned into a permanent position in June of that year at a respectable salary with attendant health benefits and matching 401K contributions. That business of mine, Chelsea Piers, well, it was not to be. Well, at least not yet and probably not ever…did I mention I'm 62? Yes I did. Probably more than once.

But I got a pretty good taste of my own place during that Saatchi run. I got hired, off to the side by a start-up company called ClickStar, an internet movie service, now gone, but promising for a minute. ClickStar offered something I was not quite able to fathom (I'm 62; I don't download). It was a service for downloading movies, still one more option of how to use your laptop or cellphone. Movies offered pretty much as soon as they were released in theatres and I got hired to write my famous one-liners to sell a movie. Right up my alley, as it were—I love movies, and it was a great gig. Paid, contractually, by retainer, an ultra-cool ten grand a month but it was a thrill for me as I got to read screenplays and see early rough cuts of films to write the lines that would encapsulate them.

But, for about a year, with an additional $120,000, thank you, I handled ClickStar and felt like an agency head with no one to answer to but Morgan Freeman—one of the partners in the venture, and I wrote a line for a bunch of forgettable films. *You Are Who You Meet*, for a Morgan film about a movie star (Mr. Freeman) who meets a woman in a supermarket in a slum while researching a film project and she changes his life in that one day. Ergo: you are who you meet and you are and we all are…

And then there was a rather obscure but hot and gone too soon movie called *Lonely Hearts* with James Gandolfini, John Travolta and Selma Hayek and Jared Leto, those last two preying on new widows and lonely women. Leto professes love for them and usurps them for their money, and then kills them. The line I wrote: *Love Can Be Murder* and the design a very Saul Bass *Anatomy of a Murder* look that in the end didn't fly because ClickStar was failing and a new guy brought in to save it which didn't happen but, the new guy, as new guys are prone to do, wanted his own team, his own choices.

But, while it lasted, it was a tiny taste of my own business and a cool hundred grand or so, but ClickStar folds and everyone moves on. I stay at Saatchi.

Saatchi.

As I began this piece, all of these full of myself pages ago, Saatchi—another short form, ad people are in a rush, impatient. Saatchi, or as the London branch of the agency is pronounced: *The Saaarrtchis.*

You find love in all the unexpected places. As of this writing, as I am about to bring this to a close, I am there twelve years. The longest lasting job I've had prior to this one was at Doyle. That lasted four and a half years. Scali, two and a half years. Sacks, one and a half. Benton and Bowles, six months—you and I see a pattern here, early jobs lasted half as long as the job before.

Ally was two, Della Femina, four. Freelance, once two years, then again seven years. Now Saatchi. All right. It's boring.

But, amazingly, it goes on.

And let me explain why that seems to be.

In the end, advertising is about results. It's about sales. It is about 'engaging the consumer'. It is about those consumers consuming. It is not about putting on a tuxedo and winning an award, fun and thrilling as all that was. It is, in the case of the brand I currently sell, Olay, women finding the product winning. And buying it.

When I started as a lowly freelancer on the brand, then a respected staffer shuffling off to Cincinnati, with my storyboards and print ads under my arm, Oil of Olay sold a respectable half a billion dollars worth of face creams and body washes and the like. Today, thanks in large part to my effort, Olay is approaching three billion dollars in world-wide sales. (Thank you, Hymo.)

Yes, we are full of ourselves with our egos and our Clios and our God knows. We celebrate ourselves and we get paid millions and, like rock stars, we have names and do drugs and we rise and we fall. And we rise.

But, frankly, I never knew how many Volkswagens my work was responsible for selling. I never did care, in those earlier years, how many people chose to go to Aamco Transmissions or buy YSL's Rive Gauche eau de toilette. When I was busy building my career, making a moderate name for myself, it was never about selling. It was about doing the work that would get me noticed and get me the next job.

Now, it is perhaps, no probably without a doubt, the

Back in the Star Again

best thing I have ever done in advertising, well, with hindsight and maturity. Now, it is best—also because it is now. Because the Olay client gives me flowers and says: "Thank you, Hy", and I get to hear things like, in quarterly reviews: "Without you, Hy, our phenomenal growth would not have ever been even remotely possible".

But, as we do, I exaggerate.

That's what we do, in advertising. Hyperbole. Exaggeration. Larger than life. Larger than anything.

Abercrombie and Fitch clothing is sold by featuring naked men. I sell Olay to women 50-plus by showing women in the 30–35 age range.

Nike does it by saying *Just Do It*.

Apple pits itself against PCs as Coke and Pepsi fought their cola wars.

American Express pays Ellen DeGeneris (as Cover Girl does, too) for her dancing in the streets to street music.

Advertising has its own language, all so often finding itself in the vernacular: *I can't believe I ate the whole thing* was written for Alka Seltzer a good thirty or more years ago. Like it was yesterday.

Yesterday: *There's an app for that,* coined like a classic.

Where's The Beef? still remembered and although cigarette advertising was banned from the airwaves many decades ago, I still remember Julie London singing *"You get a lot to like with a Marlboro…"* sexily, in the back of a black and white limousine. And then there was *Show us your Lark pack* as vivid as the black eyes for Tareyton: *I'd rather fight than switch.*

But I didn't write any of those lines or slogans.

I just plodded along, up, down, down, out, on top in a tux, and receiving flowers from a client, gratefully. And fired. And fired. And found.

Tomorrow?

Who can say.

All I can say is this is what I do.

— 2010

Back in the Star Again

Last night I had dinner at the Maidstone. It is the place where a lot of the stories in this collection were written. Rowdy Hall, too. But the Maidstone Arms, mostly, in their earlier, nautical incarnation. In the dining room, at lunch, over a period of 24 (!) years.

It's a different Maidstone now. It's colorful and jazzy and offers gravlax and herring and other Swedish-oriented fare. But the draw for me in 2010 is not the wing chair in the corner of its original front dining room where I sat and wrote *A Date With Andy*. Nor in the further inside dining room where I overheard the Christie Brinkley conversation. The draw is Scott, the bartender.

Scott is young. A lawyer taking hiatus, surfing in Montauk and tending the bar in a lime green bow tie and

Back in The Star Again

a black satin vest. He actually is a little Chippendale-y, but he's brainier. And handsomer. But just as broad in the shoulder and trim in the waist. Twenty five years old. And he thinks I'm a star. (Well, I tip big.)

When you're a writer, you're not really a star. You toil and you rewrite and you hate everything you write. "Self-conscious," I often think of my writing. "Trying too hard." But Scott says otherwise: "Hy! I read your piece on the pool guy! (*Forgiveness: Hampton Style*) and he proceeds to quote phrases from it, word for word. He even comes out from behind the bar to embrace me—be still my beating, Lipitor-enhanced heart. (I tip very big.)

But I ramble.

The fact is, being in *The East Hampton Star* has been a crowning achievement, cliché as that sounds. But it's true. As all clichés are. When I first found out I was to be published in the Star—the year was 1993, I felt a jolt, then a lift and a sense that, at long last, I was to be recognized as a SERIOUS WRITER! Advertising is anonymous. OK, I got fairly well-known by winning awards and the fact that I lasted four decades in the business and counting (see *What I Do*). But advertising is collaborative and advertising is compromise. The Star publishes me with exactly what I want to say and exactly the way I want to say it (thank you, Virginia Garrison).

The Star.

Back in the Star Again

That first story they decided to publish was *South Of Highway Robbery* way back in 1993. I don't remember where I was when I wrote it—I think at home in Amagansett shortly after the big event of the robbery occurred. But I will never forget the moment I saw it all in print.

As the Star comes out on Thursday and I wasn't scheduled to be out in the Hamptons until Friday and couldn't possibly wait, I found that it was also sold somewhere around Grand Central, not far from the Jitney stop. I was freelancing, working on M&M's at another now defunct agency that Thursday it came out. I took the day off. Went to that newsstand and bought 20 copies. Headed downtown on Lexington Avenue into a bar named South Dakota (now gone like the ad agency) and ordered a vodka tonic and sat under a light behind the bar and proceeded to read it. Each sentence, each *word* sending a charge through me.

I did it.

I did it.

Renée and Me is a different story. I sent it to the Star, the second story I ever sent to them, and heard nothing. Then a couple of weeks later, I was in Los Angeles shooting a commercial in a sound stage, when I got a call from my writing coach in New York named Cynthia. "A friend of mine in East Hampton says you're in the Star! She sent me a fax of it. It's fun!"

I freaked.

Back in The Star Again

"I *am*?! Can you send it to me? Fax it to me?"

They never notified me, the cool Star, but I loved it just the same. And it did get faxed and I savored every word. Amazed, enthralled, and just so grateful. I called a friend who lived in East Hampton and asked if he would pick up some copies for me. 20. I wanted 40. 60. I wanted to give the world hard copies of it even in our world-on-a-screen era. I wanted 80 copies. To hand them out, like a newsboy in a cap, the whole paper as it is also interesting to me to see in the Star what all else was going on around the story. (I still have most of all of those copies now. Yellowing. Crumbling. I refuse to throw any of them out.)

Now, I'm really a serious writer. Two stories, two Guestwords pieces in the Star.

A few years pass. I'm busy with fiction, another form I still write in but get nowhere with. Then, I have an incident with my pool guy and a light bulb goes off. "I'll write about this and the Star will want it," I think, the hubris, my toe now deep in the water filled with confidence. The feeling that everything I write they will now want.

Forgiveness: Hampton Style struck a nerve with people. Could be the one story that garnered the most positive reaction. It's a human piece, if I do say so myself, the human that wrote it. It seemed to herald a catharsis: the new Hy. Gentler. Forgiving. Alas, it was an isolated, if opportunistic incident. The new Hy can still be as

Back in the Star Again

unforgiving as the old Hy.

I read that piece on the 4:01 from Grand Central to East Hampton—that glorious Friday afternoon train, even with its frantic change at Jamaica. Cooler now, story three, I didn't pick up any copies in New York, but decided to wait until I got out East Friday evening. But as luck would have it, a guy with a subscription to the Star (maybe I should get one or maybe they should give me one—they don't pay for my pieces except with free copies) was seated right behind me and reading it.

"Excuse me...I'm a writer," I said. Well, I am, thanks to the Star. As an ad writer I'd always had to say I'm a copywriter. Now I can say: I'm a writer. "And I have a column in that issue you have there. Do you mind if I see that section?"

People are impressed with writers. I'm impressed that I'm a writer.

"Sure," he said, raising his eyebrows. "Which piece is yours?"

"Guestwords," I said. "The piece about me and the pool guy."

He hadn't read it yet, but handed it over. "Here. Keep it," he said, handing me the Commentary section. I didn't necessarily want to keep it. There were 20, 40, 60, 80 copies of the Star available to me in their quaint country house offices on Main Street. Besides, I wanted *him* to read it.

Back in The Star Again

"Thanks," I said and turned back around in my seat and read it. Read it twice. Read it three times. Folded it up and put it in my bag. Once home, I read it a fourth time.

Back in the Star again!

Ain't no stopping me now.

In August of 2008, I saw a work-in-progress performance of *Love, Loss and What I Wore* at the Bridgehampton Community House. It was a first look at a Delia and Nora Ephron play that is currently running off-Broadway. For me, it was fodder for my 'column'. That's how I started to think of it now. "Oh, it's not much, but I have a column in the Star," I would tell people. Humble, but thrilled. OK. So it wasn't exactly my column—Guestwords is anyone's column, but with now *My Night With Nora*, my fourth piece, I felt full of myself enough to say: I have a column. Well, it is a column. And I am featured in it. So you do the equation.

2009 was a banner year for me and the Star. Three pieces appeared from April through August.

That year, last year, I had *The Deal With Dogs, My Two Dads* (Father's Day issue) and *If You Want to Feel 100*. And let me say, with seven pieces out there, my column, really almost a column!, I have to tell you: Reading the *100* piece, sixteen years after my first story appeared there, was exactly the same exultant experience. I *am* impressed. Aren't you?

(In 2010, Puccini, Part 2 appeared. A column, for sure!)

And lastly, I wrote a piece called *The Summer of '09* about the crazy, cool and rainy summer that wasn't. I never bothered to send it to the Star and it doesn't appear here, either. Perhaps in a further edition: *Back in the Star Again, Again?* a sequel, as it were. But a friend of mine suggested I put a book together. This book together. He even inspired the title. The title should be followed by an exclamation point to describe the utter euphoria, the thrill of it all, that I am thought of as a writer. Recognized for something I've been doing for over 40 years and yet, when told I'm back in the Star again, I get teary and I walk to the beach with a copy of the Star under my arm, look up at the heavens, read the story again and marvel at the idea that 40 years on: *I am a writer.*

There is nothing else I would rather be.

— 2010